ONE PUTT

ONE PUTT

THE ULTIMATE GUIDE TO PERFECT PUTTING

KEN BROWN

hamlyn

CONTENTS

FOREWORD

In my mind golf has always been much more an art than a science, this is certainly true when it comes to putting. Everyone plays their best with flair, instinct, feel and touch.

To putt well, like anything in life, you need to understand the basics. *One Putt* will explain just that.

Ken Brown charmed the ball into the hole with his old hickory-shafted putter, he was one of the best.

Let a Picasso with the putter teach you simply to hole more putts.

Play well,

Seve

March 2011

Seve kindly wrote this for me when I told him I was thinking about writing a putting book. We played together, commentated together and in his later years became friends. Without these words I am not sure I would have transformed my folder of notes into what I hope is a book he would have enjoyed reading. He was an artist who inspired me, his fellow pros and golfers around the world.

Seve salutes a One Putt at St Andrews to win the 1984 Open.

INTRODUCTION

The summer of 1969 saw Tony Jacklin's Open Championship triumph at Royal Lytham & St. Annes. I was only 12 at the time and hadn't been playing golf very long, but it was then I started to dream about following in his footsteps and becoming a professional golfer.

I wasn't powerfully built and when I saw the way some of the older lads hit the ball I knew that to compete with them I would need to keep up using other means. This meant having to develop a really top-notch short game. My home club provided me with an ideal training ground. With its tight fairways and tiny, subtly contoured greens you would struggle to find a better course than Harpenden Common for honing your short game. Armed with this tailor-made environment and a single-minded, unrelenting determination I set out to become the best putter I possibly could.

In August 1974 I was still at school studying for A levels and had whittled my handicap down to two. I felt the time was right to take up golf full time so I left school to join Graham Dove, at Verulam Golf Club, as his assistant pro. It was a dream come true, to be able to focus full time on improving my game and to be earning £10 per week to do it! I didn't realize then just how quickly my golf would take me even further. Just three years later I was representing Great Britain and Ireland in the Ryder Cup matches at Royal Lytham & St. Annes. At 20 I was one of the youngest ever to play and about to take on a team including Jack Nicklaus and Tom Watson. I still wasn't relying on power to compete and I certainly wasn't a long hitter compared to some of the players I would be facing; it was my short game that led me to the biggest team competition in golf. The long evenings I spent putting on the greens at the Common were really starting to pay off!

With a year's experience of the professional game under my belt I found myself in contention during the final round of the 1978 Irish Open. Stood on the final tee at Portmarnock, with Ireland's John O'Leary and 15,000 Dubliners hoping for a home winner, we both held a slender one-stroke advantage over Seve, the clubhouse leader, who had just shot a magical 65. To this day I'm still reminded about the way I finished. I opened with a low swirling hook, a 3-wood that sent the ball straight into the tangled, sun-bleached rough on the left side of the fairway. I chose an 8-iron for my second shot and addressed the ball, hoping to scuttle it somewhere near the green. I didn't. I shanked my approach so it rocketed straight into a grandstand, sending the spectators running for cover as the ball rattled around the metalwork. Even after a free drop I was still left with what seemed a near-impossible situation. My next challenge was a 70-yard pitch from a hard and trodden lie to a pin cut only a few paces over two yawning pot bunkers guarding the elevated green. I opened the face of my sand-wedge and made a crisp three-quarter swing, sending the ball skyward; it landed with a puff of sand just past the bunkers and trickled down the slope to within 15 feet, a good shot, but there was still work to be done. John O'Leary had a 20-foot par putt and much to his supporters' disappointment he missed, leaving my door open. Even having One Putted all but one of the greens so far on the back nine, I still needed to sink another to secure my first win on Tour. Confident I had chosen the right line, all I needed to do was repeat the same basics I had been working on since my days as a junior. I relied on my routine, kept my head still and trusted my stroke. ONE PUTT, I was the Irish Open Champion!

The old hickory putter rolls another One Putt into the hole.

Later that year 78 per cent of the European Tour players voted me the best putter on Tour. I just loved putting. The more I studied and worked at trying to get the little white ball into the 4¼-inch hole the more fascinating and entertaining it became. Over the next 20 years I spent hours experimenting, battling frustration and backache and rejoicing in eureka moments while trying to master the unmasterable.

In this book, I share some basic fundamentals that everyone can learn to help develop a consistent, repeatable, dependable and reliable putting stroke. This updated edition of *One Putt* now includes an insight into how Georgia Hall created the right mindset to become the 2018 Women's British Open Champion, some wonderful new photographs of Tiger Woods, Rickie Fowler and Jason Day, a technical review of some new putters and recent rule changes.

Read on to find out *all* you need to know to One Putt!

THE PUTTING LADDER

One Putt is a concise and easily followed field guide to everything you need to know to hole more putts. You will gain most from this book by starting at the bottom of the ladder and climbing up rung by rung in its logical order.

Start with my advice on how to choose the right putter – one that you will fall in love with – then move on to the basics from grip to set-up. Next is help with reading greens and picking the line and pace. The act of putting begins with the set-up routine and how to address the ball consistently time after time, to achieve a repeatable sound stroke. With a little practice on the putting green or your carpet at home, the basics – manageable to everyone – will fall into place.

Something all good putters have is touch! Touch can't be taught – it can only be acquired – so the next step up the ladder helps you develop judgement of pace with touch and feel. Improving this is often overlooked in the search of the perfect stroke. To putt well touch is as important as technique.

Final steps up the ladder include practical simple tips and drills that have been gathered over the years, winning on both the European and PGA Tours, playing in five Ryder Cups and watching the world's best while working as a commentator for Sky, BBC, Fox Sport and the Golf Channel. These will give you my 'Ken on the Course' tips ('Brownie Points' for Fox Sport viewers), pointers and the odd story, to make practice more profitable and enjoyable.

Take yourself to the top of the ladder …
and relish the joy of more One Putts!

THE PUTTING PIE

You may marvel at how some people putt. Your aunty may have holed out with 'a stick of rhubarb and a walnut' on *her* day, but if she wanted to putt *consistently* she would need to get the basics right.

Putting is the easiest department of your game to improve. The golfing pie (below) clearly illustrates what a big part of your game it is. Putting is almost half the game, and half of those putts are under 6 feet and all performed with the same club.

No matter what sport you play, there is great satisfaction in taking aim at something and hitting your target. The joy the footballer gets as his shot hits the back of the goal is like a golf ball disappearing, rattling into the bottom of the cup.

Just how good are the very best modern-day pros in the world? Statistics from the PGA Tour show the cumulative number of putts, from the 2008–2019 seasons,

hit by the players ranked No. 1 in each length category (see below). There are two interesting observations from these statistics. Firstly, the best putters from 3 feet never missed. Unbelievable! Secondly, the chances of them facing a 3-foot putt are roughly 15 times more likely than a 6-footer and nearly 20 times greater than a 10-footer.

Therefore improving holing out from 3 feet is going to have the greatest benefit to your score. Both Jason Day and Charl Schwartzel won majors in years that they holed 100 per cent of putts from 3 feet.

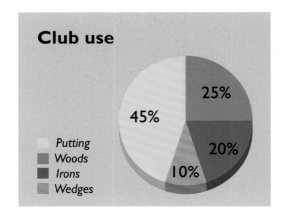

Club use

- 25%
- 45%
- 20%
- 10%

Putting
Woods
Irons
Wedges

PGA Tour 2008–2019

Range	Per cent	Putts hit	Putts holed
3 feet	100	9,450	9,450
6 feet	85	664	567
10 feet	63	438	275

MY US TOUR INITIATION

Back in the 1970s if you made the Great Britain and Ireland Ryder Cup team the US PGA Tour gave you three precious exemptions to cross the Atlantic and play with the 'big boys' of golf. After my 1977 Ryder Cup debut at Royal Lytham & St. Annes I took advantage of this opportunity, in January 1978. I arrived into Tucson airport late on New Year's Eve naively expecting a courtesy car to be waiting. In its obvious absence I called the Country Club, host of the Tucson Open, and they kindly sent one of the members to collect me. The generous, jovial man dropped me off at my accommodation, one of the condos on the course, before he returned to the festivities going on in the clubhouse. American hospitality at its best! When looking out of the window the following morning, I couldn't believe the blue skies, perfect fairways and the sun shining; it was like a golfer's equivalent of Disneyland.

After missing the cut in Tucson and spending my 21st birthday watching the rest of it on TV I headed to the Phoenix Open, hoping for better luck and excited to be in a field with some of my heroes – Arnie Palmer, Lee Trevino, Johnny Miller, Tom Watson and Tony Jacklin. My opening two rounds – my only two – were in the company of Gary McCord and Fuzzy Zoeller, neither of whom I had heard of before. They didn't pause for breath through 18 holes, talking constantly about anything and everything, and both were very funny. This was completely new to me, the crowds loved it and it made me wonder why they didn't take their golf more seriously. On virtually every hole Fuzzy would tee up on the left of the tee blocks and Gary on the right simultaneously and still chatting. Fuzzy would hit a draw and Gary a fade with barely a pause between them; it was almost like a Laurel and Hardy comedy sketch.

Despite all the banter both were outstanding putters, but it was Fuzzy who really caught my eye with the unnerving way he nonchalantly holed out from inside 6 feet. He walked up to the ball, whistling to himself without a care in the world, had a casual couple of practice strokes and then struck the ball with such confidence that it seemed to glide rather than roll towards the hole. In the 36 holes I played with him he didn't come close to not hitting one dead centre into the back of the cup; the hole could have been half the size and it would have made no difference. Fuzzy won the Masters the following year, and it really drove home to me that the essence of good putting was reliably holing out from short range, something that Fuzzy made look so easy. The first step up the ladder is choosing the right putter so let's get started.

chapter one

CHOOSING A PUTTER

The more comfortable you feel with your choice of putter, the more likely you are to hole putts.

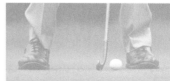

A CRUCIAL CHOICE

For hundreds of years, from the early club makers to the modern high-tech manufacturers, the quest has continued to find the best putting implement.

There are thousands of different putters, each one being sold with the promise of success. Each has its own advantage, from the old hickory-bladed putter to the latest grooved, high moment of inertia, face-balanced, milled, alignment-aided modern masterpiece. Putter design has always been a blend of art and science; the one thing all putters have in common is a 'sweet spot'. This is a point on the face where the club will not twist when you strike the ball.

Choosing the best putter gives you the foundation you need on which to build your basic putting skills. Just as you would not want to drive a car with unbalanced wheels, it is best to hone your skill with a putter that is set up to give YOU maximum control of distance and direction.

The club has to be your friend – you have to like the way it LOOKS and FEELS.

Every putter is unique; choose the one that works for you.

MASTERLY SUCCESS FOR MY PUTTER

In return for some feedback, putter manufacturers would often give me their latest design to try. During the 1989 PGA Tour's Honda Classic at Eagle Trace Golf Club in Florida, I was on the putting green experimenting with a TaylorMade TPA XVIII that had been made to my spec. Nick Faldo approached and asked if he could have a go with it. It was 34 inches long, one inch shorter than his own, which he felt allowed his arms to hang down more naturally at address. I lent the TaylorMade putter to him, and a few weeks later he put it into his bag for his final round at Augusta National – if only I hadn't, it might now be Sir Ken!

Nick Faldo holes his putt on the 11th green at Augusta National in 1989 to beat Scott Hoch in the play-off and win his first green jacket! 'THANK YOU!'

Regardless of what putter you choose there are a number of key factors you must consider. You also need to understand some of the advantages and disadvantages of different designs.

The following factors are critical in making the right decision – LENGTH, LIE, LOFT and WEIGHT – and then your personal selection of design.

LENGTH

By using the right length of putter shaft you can assume the correct posture, which helps get your hands and arms flowing together with the putter.

To decide on the shaft length, you need to experiment with several different ones. Although your height will affect your choice, the most important factor is feeling comfortable when addressing the ball.

Most standard putters are 33–36 inches long. Try a slightly shorter one initially as this makes it much easier to adopt the correct posture at address and ensure your eyes are directly over the ball.

Testing the length

The left hand and arm should fall into a comfortable position such that the putter shaft and the forearm have the feeling of working together without tension.

Ideally your hands and arms should hang naturally when about to putt.

LIE

The lie of a putter is the angle between the sole and the putter shaft. It is very difficult to putt with any consistency if the lie is more than a couple of degrees out.

Understanding the lie

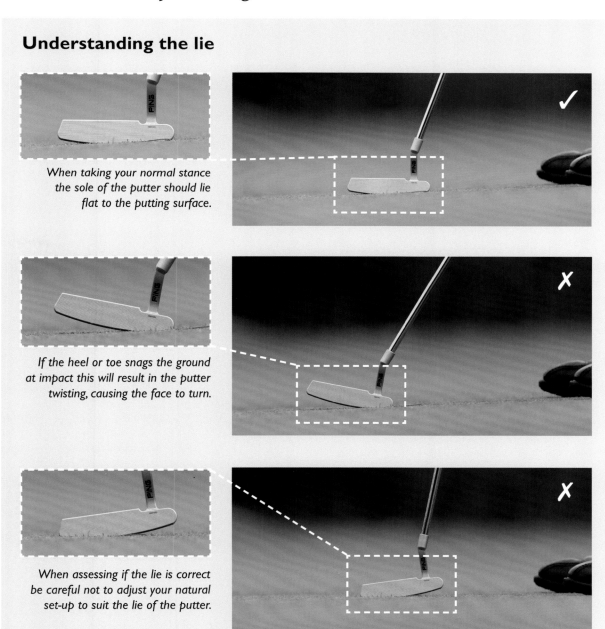

When taking your normal stance the sole of the putter should lie flat to the putting surface.

If the heel or toe snags the ground at impact this will result in the putter twisting, causing the face to turn.

When assessing if the lie is correct be careful not to adjust your natural set-up to suit the lie of the putter.

LOFT

This is often overlooked in putter selection. It is obvious with irons that the loft affects the trajectory of the shot, but you might think that a putter does not require any loft as the objective is to roll the ball along the ground.

However when the ball comes to rest on the green it will settle in its own depression no matter how short the grass is. A little loft helps lift the ball from where it has settled.

Over the last hundred years the loft on putters has gradually been reduced as putting surfaces have become smoother,

with improved maintenance. Bobby Jones (winner of the Grand Slam in 1930) used a putter called Calamity Jane, which had 8 degrees of loft, most modern putters now have 1–5 degrees. Club greens are generally slower than tournament greens so loft becomes a little more important.

A golf ball

○ 1.68 inches in diameter.

○ No more than 1.62 ounces in weight.

○ Even if the grass is cut tight, approximately 8 per cent of a golf ball sits in its own little depression.

A quick visual check of your loft

This is a quick way to check how much loft you have on your putter face. Hold the face against a flat surface and see how far the top of the grip is leaning away from the perpendicular. Every inch that it leans forward roughly equates to one degree of loft. Using a putter that is set up correctly for you is far more important than its design.

Once putted, the ball will typically skid for the first 15–18 per cent of its travel before the friction from the ground causes it to roll. Without the correct loft, the ball will skid further or bounce, meaning that it will take longer to make contact with the grass and to achieve optimum roll. By reducing the skidding distance, you will be able to judge the putt's pace and line better. All research and experience suggest that at impact the ideal loft to deliver to the ball is 2–4 degrees. Without the correct loft you will need to make adjustments to your stroke to create it, and this will inevitably introduce inconsistency.

The only thing that causes the ball to roll is its friction with the ground. The sooner the ball starts rolling the better it holds its line; thus, judgement of speed becomes easier. The effective loft at impact has a large influence on this.

A little loft will help get your rock rolling.

Choosing the correct loft

The right loft varies from player to player depending how the ball is addressed. The further your 'hands are ahead' of the putter face the more loft is required (see diagram below).

With a 34-inch putter, the loft will effectively be reduced by one degree for approximately each inch your hands are ahead of the putter face. So for example, if your hands are 1 inch ahead and you want a final loft of three degrees at impact, you would need a putter face with four degrees of loft.

The simple guide below illustrates how your hands' position affects the effective loft of the putter. A neutral position at address will not affect the loft.

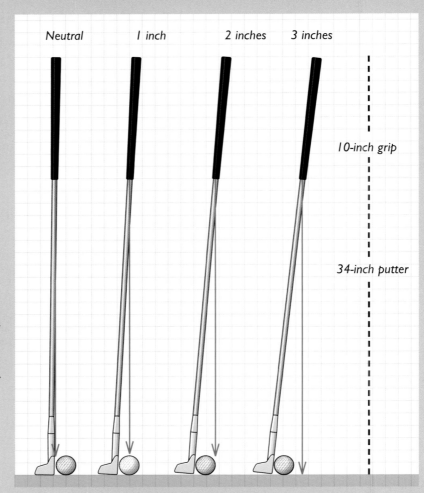

Neutral   1 inch   2 inches   3 inches

10-inch grip

34-inch putter

The red line helps you visualize how far your hands are ahead of the face when you address the ball.

Here's how it looks
when it's all finished.
    The correct length,
lie and loft get the
putter shaft, your
hands and forearms
working as a unit
and your eye line is
directly over the ball.

WEIGHT

How heavy the clubhead feels when it is swung is known as its swing-weight, and this is measured on a scale that ranges from A to G, each letter having ten graduations. Most regular putters sold are between D2 and E5.

To give you a feel for the swing-weight try holding your putter by the head and make a few strokes with the putter upside down. If you then turn it back to normal and make some more strokes, you will immediately feel the swing-weight and how it enhances your awareness of the clubhead.

Ball speed is determined by the weight and speed of the putter head.

My advice would always be to choose a swing-weight between D5 and E2, which will give you a heavier feel in the head. Your putting stroke is just a shortened

Relative swing-weights

This table shows the correlation between the putter length and the clubhead weight and how it affects the swing-weight.	Putter length	Head weight	Swing-weight	Head weight	Swing-weight
	35 inches	330 g	D5	340 g	D9
	34 inches	350 g	D5	360 g	D9
	33 inches	370 g	D5	380 g	D9

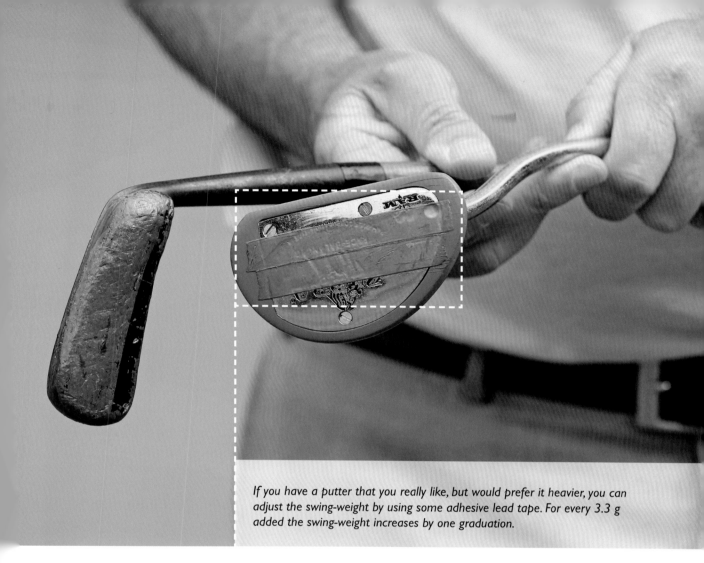

If you have a putter that you really like, but would prefer it heavier, you can adjust the swing-weight by using some adhesive lead tape. For every 3.3 g added the swing-weight increases by one graduation.

version of a full swing; the extra weight will help the rhythm and general flow of your stroke, making judgement of distance a little easier.

In general, a heavier feel in the head than a standard putter tends to give you more help on short putts, while a slightly lighter one makes it a little easier to apply a more delicate touch on long putts.

Now you have the essentials – length, lie, loft and weight – it is time to consider your own personal preferences.

THE SWEET SPOT

Every putter has a sweet spot; when the ball is struck from here the putter face will not twist. Putters of the same weight, when struck from the sweet spot, will produce virtually the same results regardless of design.

Striking the ball on the sweet spot is at the heart of putting well. The sweet spot may already be marked by the manufacturer, but if this is not the case it may be helpful to know where it is. To check this, hold the putter off the ground with the putter shaft at the angle you would normally address the ball, then tap the clubface until you find the spot where it doesn't twist. The sweet spot position needs to be tested both across and up and down the face. There will only be one small spot that the club will not twist; keep checking until you are confident that the face is stable when tapped. You may also discover that the tap sounds different when you hit the sweet spot as opposed to either side of it. If it helps, you can mark the sweet spot on the

The more often you hit the ball from the sweet spot the better you will putt.

The sweet spot here is marked with three dots.

Use a tee or a key to tap the face.

top of the leading edge, first with a pencil to make sure of your accuracy and then with an indelible pen.

The importance of striking the ball from the sweet spot will be explained on page 101.

The sweet spot
is not always in the centre
of the clubface.

MOMENT OF INERTIA

Moment of inertia (MOI) is an important consideration when choosing your putter.

In simple terms MOI is a clubhead's resistance to twisting when it hits the ball. If you strike the ball from any part of the face other than the sweet spot, the head will twist, although a putter with high MOI will twist less. The weight of the putter also has an effect on MOI. If you have two putters that are of identical design and specification, but one is heavier, it will have a slightly higher MOI and therefore will twist less.

A higher MOI will be of most benefit to higher handicap golfers.

What is MOI?

I hope the cartoon analogy shown here will help you understand MOI. The bars and weights are the same in these two illustrations:

○ The bar with the weights closer together will be easier to twist, making it less forgiving.

○ The bar with the weights positioned at the ends will be more difficult to twist.

Lower MOI

Higher MOI

When choosing a putter always remember that
the higher the MOI, the more resistant it is to twisting
if you miss the sweet spot.

Putter with its weight distributed to increase MOI

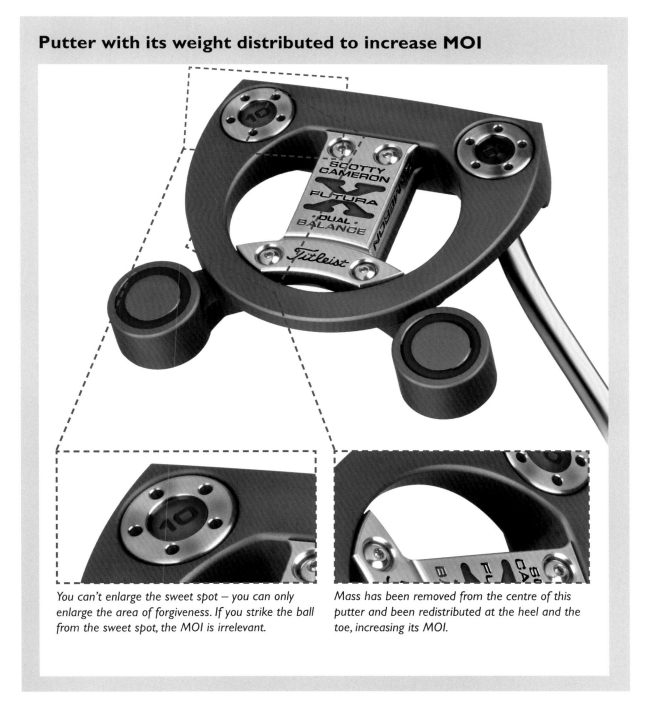

You can't enlarge the sweet spot – you can only enlarge the area of forgiveness. If you strike the ball from the sweet spot, the MOI is irrelevant.

Mass has been removed from the centre of this putter and been redistributed at the heel and the toe, increasing its MOI.

INSERTS, GROOVES AND SOUNDS OFF THE FACE

Originally putter inserts were introduced to try to soften both the feel and sound of the modern golf ball, which had become progressively harder.

Recently, manufacturers have softened the covering on a golf ball, but despite this, inserts are still sometimes used to change the feel of the ball off the clubface.

Inserts are also sometimes used to distribute the weight of the putter. This is done by removing some of the weight from the centre of the clubface and replacing it with a lighter insert, giving the putter a marginally higher moment of inertia.

Sound off the putter face

The sound the ball makes when leaving the putter face can have a significant impact on how the putter feels. There are only two senses that give you feedback as to whether you have made contact with the sweet spot and how hard you have hit the ball. One is the feeling through the grip to your hands, while the other is the sound of the ball coming off the putter face. The sound is essential in

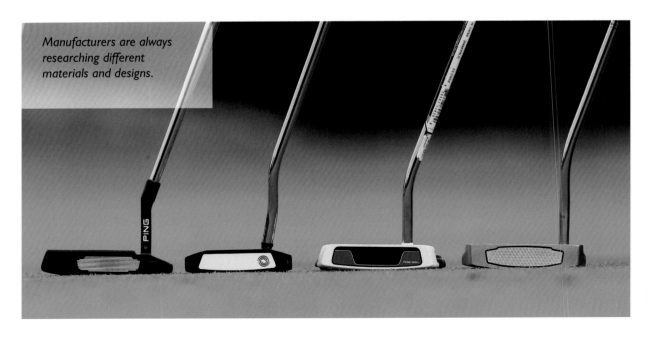

Manufacturers are always researching different materials and designs.

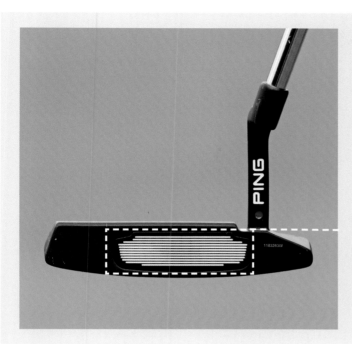

Grooves on a putter

Grooves may reduce the speed that a ball comes off the clubface, meaning that it will not roll as far. The deeper any grooves are, the softer the impact feels and the less distance the ball travels. Ping developed a putter face with slightly deeper grooves in the centre and shallower ones on the heel and toe, to get a more even ball speed across more of the face.

knowing whether you have struck the putt correctly.

Ping named their putters based on the sound the ball made when it was hit! This was one of the factors that made the putters so successful. To sum up, inserts can change the feel and the sound the ball makes off the clubface.

Listen — the sound will reveal how the ball has been struck.

BALANCE

Different putters balance in different ways depending on their design. Face balanced and toe balanced are just ways to describe the two ends of the spectrum.

To find out how a putter is balanced, rest its shaft across the palm of your hand and notice how the putter face naturally wants to hang. On a standard toe-balanced putter, the toe will point down to the ground, while on a face-balanced putter the clubface will point up towards the sky. Ultimately the only thing that controls the clubface is you yourself. Therefore, however the face is balanced – face, toe or in between – select the putter that is best matched to your particular stroke.

Toe balance

The toe-balanced putter is better suited to the golfer who has more of an arc in their swing path. This tends to be those who are less experienced, although there are plenty of elite players who have great success with toe-balanced putters. This style of putter is still the most widely used.

Face balance

Here, the centre of gravity is in line with the axis of the shaft, which results in the clubface pointing skyward. The idea of face balancing is to help the clubface resist rotation during the stroke. Therefore a face-balanced putter is more suitable for players who have less arc in their swing path. Among the world's best players there is a mix of stroke types between the two types of putter.

PUTTER FACE DEPTH

The depth of the putter face is often overlooked.
Generally the deeper it is, the higher the sweet spot
will be from the putter's sole.

This has a significant bearing on how a putter is stroked. In order to hit the ball from the sweet spot with a shallow-face putter you will need to make an adjustment to your stroke to return the face to a higher position (see below). No compensation is required for the deeper

face putter. My advice, especially for a higher handicap golfer, is to use a slightly deeper face, eliminating the need for any manipulation. Interestingly, the maximum depth allowed by the Rules is 2½ inches.

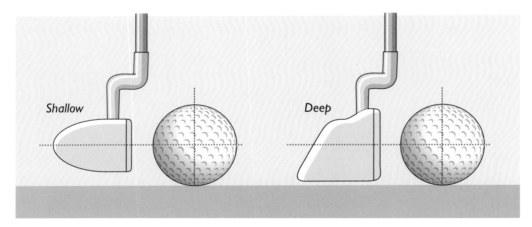

At impact, the shallow-face putter no longer brushes the grass as it did at address. The deep-face putter returns to the same position.

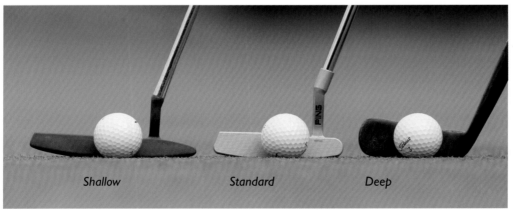

A 'ball's eye' view of these putter faces.

SHAFT FLEX

The shaft is probably the least considered factor when choosing a putter. Even pros normally choose their putters based on other attributes. There is no evidence that the shaft's flexibility affects the putter's performance. The first school of thought suggests a stiffer shaft provides stability and more control, while the second theory is that more flex allows the putter head to release, thereby giving a little more feel.

My trusty old hickory is flexible and has the most wonderful feel – you can almost hear the putter sing from the vibrations resonating up the shaft.

Stiff shaft

The shorter the putter shaft is, generally the stiffer it is, yet the stiffer the shaft the less feel of the head you have. Shafts have tended to get stiffer as head weights and longer lengths have become popular.

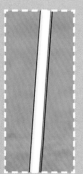

Flexible shaft

Flexible shafts enable you to feel the head a little more easily. Some older putters, such as the Bullseye and the Wilson 8802, had softer shafts to make up for the lighter head weights.

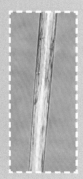

GRIPS AND GRIP ALIGNMENT

The grip is the only part of the putter with which you have contact and therefore has a major influence on how the putter feels. It is available in boundless different thicknesses, shapes, weights, lengths and materials; the choice is very personal.

Like putter heads, grips are continually being researched and developed to find the ultimate all rounder.

The lighter the grip is, the heavier the putter head will feel, and vice versa. I would recommend that you steer away from heavy grips unless the clubhead is specifically designed for one.

Time for a change

One thing is for certain, if the grip is getting old and shiny, it is time to replace it. If you can be with the pro when your grip is changed it can be custom fitted to suit you. A new grip on a favourite putter can change the whole swing feel and bring the putter back to life.

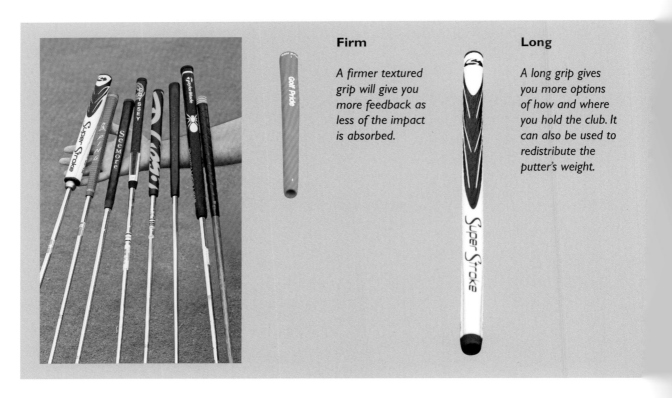

Firm

A firmer textured grip will give you more feedback as less of the impact is absorbed.

Long

A long grip gives you more options of how and where you hold the club. It can also be used to redistribute the putter's weight.

Grip alignment

Many putter grips are shaped to assist the correct positioning of your hands and to help you line up the putter. The vast majority of grips have a flat front which, when fitted properly, should ideally be at right angles to the putter face.

Your grip may have some identifying features which you can use as reminders of where your hands should be positioned. I used one of the joins on a leather grip to put my right forefinger on or the 'N' of Ping to place my left thumb … watch Tiger do this!

Thin

Thin grips are generally held more in the fingers, giving you the most sensitive touch.

Thick

Thicker grips reduce the influence of your fingers and wrists, allowing your arms and shoulders to take more control of the stroke. The Rules limit the cross-section of the grip to 1¾ inches.

Soft

A softer grip tends to be held more lightly, thereby enhancing feel and rhythm, yet it cushions the impact of the strike, which may give you less feedback.

TRY BEFORE YOU BUY

On many occasions I have looked at a new putter and thought 'this looks perfect'. But would you buy a new car without testing it? Nor should you get your credit card out for an untested putter.

To make your trial as effective as possible it is a good idea to set up an objective comparison against your existing wand. Do this test by taking both to the putting green, together with five tees and fifteen balls. If possible pick a time when the green is freshly cut, running true and not too much slope around the cup.

Using the tee pegs, set up your test track by positioning the pegs 3, 6, 9, 12 and 15 feet from the hole. Most putters are about 3 feet long, which can help with measuring out. Try to avoid walking or standing on the line of each putt.

Hit three balls from each position with the new putter and count how many you hole, then do the same with your existing one. Complete two or

three circuits keeping count and see how they compare. Once you have finished the circuit, hit a few longer putts too, to see how they feel.

A little head-to-head course gives your test a competitive edge. It is very effective practice … and you will find out which putter gives the most One Putts.

This one looks like it might be a keeper!

THE RIGHT PUTTER COULD WIN YOU THE MASTERS

I reached the Riviera Country Club, Los Angeles early on in the 1985 PGA Tour season with a distinctly cold putter. I was definitely in the hunt for a new runner. Chatting in the locker room to the US pro Clarence Rose, he proudly showed me two new weapons he had just taken delivery of from the renowned club maker T.P. Mills. Truett P. Mills had been a pioneer in handcrafted putters since the 1960s and he was regarded as the father of putter design. He was the first to hand-mill heads and mark the sweet spot, and he also engraved the owner's initials onto the putter – these two beauties had the initials C.R.

Clarence, a true gent, offered me the heavier of his two new putters on the understanding that if I didn't use it I would return it. It stayed in my bag for the following few weeks until I played a practice round with Bernhard Langer who asked if he could give it a try. The T.P. Mills, bearing Clarence's initials, found its third home and within a few weeks was holing a crucial putt which tested both nerve and talent on the 71st green at Augusta National. This put

Bernhard ahead of his playing partner, Seve, and paved his way to the Butler Cabin to put on his first green jacket.

I am not sure the putter was ever returned to its rightful owner, but it certainly put Bernhard and T.P. Mills firmly on the map. Bernhard said he liked it for its little offset head and for its soft shaft with some flex adding to its feel. Its soft-milled putter head was ideal for very fast greens and its perfect lie gave Bernhard a comfy link between the shaft and his forearms.

LOOKING AFTER YOUR PUTTER

Once you have found the perfect putter it goes without saying that it's worth protecting, just as you would with any other important investment.

❍ Any little knocks or nicks can be distracting to the eye, and in the wrong place may affect the performance.

❍ Keep the grip fresh and clean by using a soft nail brush, some diluted gentle detergent and warm water.

❍ Similarly clean the putter face, removing any grass marks you may have picked up when putting from the fringe.

❍ I used to remove any labels from the shaft so as not to distract the eyes.

❍ When travelling, place the putter into the centre of your golf bag. The most precious club needs the greatest protection; use a cover.

This is the cover that has protected my hickory since my 20th birthday. Look after your putter like a friend and it will look after you!

HOW I CHOSE MY PUTTER

You can still just see Bert's teeth marks.

In 1974, just before I turned pro, I was rummaging through a golf bag full of secondhand clubs and spotted a tatty, old, hickory-shafted putter. I immediately took a shine to it. The rusty offset head had the perfect loft and lie. It was the ideal length and the hickory shaft had such a nice feel. 'How much do you want for this?' I asked George Hamshaw, the pro at Redbourn Golf Club. 'You can have it' was the response. George, being an entrepreneur, did not give much away. 'Thank you.' I walked out of the shop before he could change his mind. My 'new' putter was made around 1900 and had no identification marks on at all; it was completely plain. After giving it a go I realized that it needed some tender, loving care so I took it to Fred Robson, the pro at Harpenden Golf Club, who was sage-like when it came to club repairs. He wound on a soft leather grip and added a lump of lead, which he skilfully shaped to the back of the putter. It now felt PERFECT! So perfect that I asked my mum to make a sheath-like cover to stop it being knocked in my bag. The hickory putter travelled round the world in its warm coat. It met presidents, played Ryder Cups, suffered a broken shaft in Zambia and was with me when I won my first Tour title in Ireland.

In my early years on Tour it was always valuable to get a practice round with a more senior player. On a blazing hot and humid afternoon at the St Jude Classic in Memphis, Bert Yancey asked if he could join me for a knock. He was a seven-time winner on the PGA Tour and as a lad I watched him nearly win the Masters a couple of times on TV. On the first green, his blue eyes lit up as he spotted me taking my trusty wand out of its scabbard. In a flash his meat-cleaver hands wrapped around it and gave it a frantic energetic waggle, saying: 'Oooh, that feels good.' 'Be careful, you will break it,' I said quickly. Next he ran the shaft under his nose as if it was a cigar: 'Oooh, it smells good too.' Alarmingly, next it was in his mouth and I could hear his teeth crunching into the grain of the shaft. At that very moment there was a loud bang of thunder; grabbing my club, we both headed back to the 'safety' of the clubhouse. That is why I called my putter Bert; his teeth marks are still in the shaft. It has still got the same grip and I still use the old putter cover my mum made. Over the years many other putters have found their way into the bag, but Bert will always be my first love!

Sadly, Bert Yancey, Fred and my dear mum are no longer with us, but Bert is still going strong, more than a hundred years later.

PUTTERS AND THEIR FEATURES

There are so many putters to choose from, but they all started from the same humble beginnings. Let's have a look at how putters have evolved through the years and some of the landmark designs and features that made them so popular.

Blade putter with a hickory shaft

This is the most basic putter design and it dates back to the early days of the game. The feedback that its simple blade gives as to where you have struck the ball is second-to-none; despite its centuries-old design, it is rarely bettered.

Features

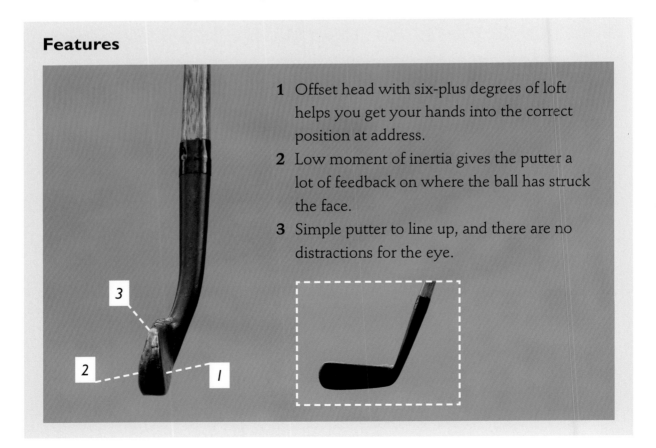

1 Offset head with six-plus degrees of loft helps you get your hands into the correct position at address.
2 Low moment of inertia gives the putter a lot of feedback on where the ball has struck the face.
3 Simple putter to line up, and there are no distractions for the eye.

Blade putter

This is a Ping Zero putter that was given to me in 1978 at their factory in Scottsdale, Arizona. It is an early adaptation of a blade putter with the weight spread around the head, adding to its MOI and lowering the centre of gravity. The clubhead was cast from a mould rather than being forged from a piece of steel.

Features

1 Offset head.
2 Grooved face.
3 Peripherally weighted, increasing its MOI.
4 Heel-shafted, toe-hang putter.

Ping Anser

The grandaddy of modern putters, designed in 1966 by the golfing visionary Karsten Solheim. His original sketches, which have fairly recently been found, were done on the dust jacket of a 78 rpm record. Almost certainly the bestselling putter in the history of golf and Seve's putter of choice for many of his wins. Its fundamental design principles are copied to this day.

Features

This is a late 1960s' example that Slazenger distributed in the UK and stamped 'Jack Nicklaus'.

1 'Plumber's neck' offset head.

2 Flexible shaft (a feature of the early Ansers) softened the feel.

3 Heel/toe weighting, giving it higher moment of inertia.

4 Sound slot that gave it the unique sound – the 'ping' – and feel.

5 Cast head.

A VISIT TO SEVE

I went to interview Seve in July 2010 for the BBC; sadly it was his last ever interview. Although he had been unwell for some time he was keen to meet and send a message to his many fans around the world.

Flying out to Bilbao on easyJet I found myself sitting next to Rafael Nadal who had won Wimbledon the day before, a surprising start to a poignant day. Rafael kindly wrote his friend a note filling nearly a side of A4 in Spanish, which I took with me.

Preparation for any interview is vital, and this was one that was difficult to plan for. I didn't know if it would take place until the last minute, nor how Seve would manage, nor if it would last ten minutes or an hour. In fact we chatted for more than two hours. The day was full of emotion, a legend who was having treatment for brain cancer and wanting to share his story. The bravery he showed throughout his many victories shone through as he recounted highlights of his career.

Seve showed me around his house and garden, some of which was transformed into an 11-hole, par-three course, as well as the garage containing his prized cars. Phil, his labrador, named after Phil Mickelson, looked on as the camera crew filed past. Going into his golf office was like entering an Aladdin's cave; it was full of clubs that had been instrumental in his success. I asked if he had the Anser he had used to win the Open at St Andrews in 1984. Who will ever forget his salute to the crowd after holing the winning putt? In his search he pulled out the Toney Penna 3-wood he had used to play out of the 18th fairway bunker in the 1983 Ryder Cup matches at PGA National – a shot still talked about today, which helped him halve his match with Fuzzy Zoeller. Sadly though, the original 1984 St Andrews Anser was not to be found, but we did uncover a bag full of golden-

headed Pings, which are sent to players to commemorate any win using one of their putters. I told Seve that nowadays major winners receive solid gold replicas, rather than the gold-plated one given out in our day. His eyes lit up, he smiled a Seve smile!

Odyssey two-ball putter

This putter was the amalgamation of a number of clever design features. The idea of using a row of balls to help the golfer aim the putter was originally developed by the 'professor of putting' Dave Pelz. On the right is Pelz's prototype with plastic-moulded balls, which he gave me in the mid-1980s – perhaps it should be in a museum dedicated to putter development history. Years later Odyssey used the ball line idea in their own design.

Dave Pelz's hand-crafted original.

When selecting a putter that has any sort of alignment aid, from the simple dot on the top edge to the elaborate Odyssey design (below), choose the one that gives you the most confidence visually.

Features

1 Two balls help with your aim.
2 Face-balanced.
3 Peripheral weighting increases the moment of inertia.
4 At address the putter head sits comfortably behind the ball.

TaylorMade Spider Putter

After first arriving on the market in 2008, the Spider Putter has evolved. The Spider mallet-headed putter below combines a lot of high-tech features and seems a long way removed from the simple blade hewn from a lump of metal. The centre is made from a lightweight, 15 g carbon composite core with a heavier 320 g outer frame, increasing the MOI. Manufacturers, recognizing that the correct aiming of the putter is the most important aspect of putting, spend a lot of time researching alignment aids. On this putter, the white line helps with aim.

Modern designs, materials and consistency of manufacture make holing putts easier.

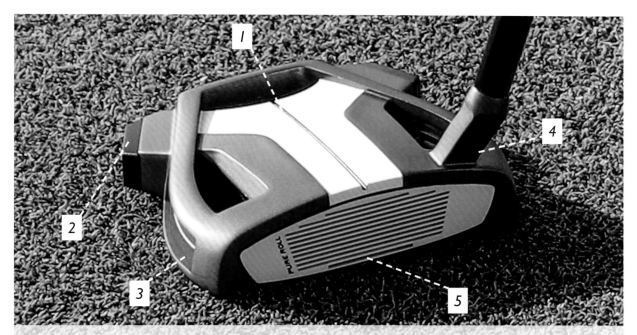

1 Simple white sight line helps with alignment and marks the position of the sweet spot.

2 Weight points spread the centre of gravity, increasing stability in the same way as a wider wheel base does on a car.

3 Compact head sits well and is pleasing to the eye.

4 Slant neck hosel.

5 Thicker insert reduces the sound at impact.

The Scotty

For more than 20 years, Tiger Woods has had one favourite putter. So favourite, in fact, he doesn't even own a back-up. Putter maker Scotty Cameron has produced more than a hundred others for Woods, but none has taken its place. Not tempted by anything new, shiny, unblemished or more modern looking, he has been loyal to 'The Scotty' which is now showing its age with some characterful scrapes and dents across its face.

After a lean spell on the greens in 1999 Woods, fastidious about putter design (especially the weight, sound and feel),

asked Cameron for a Newport 2 with the sweet spot at the absolute centre, to be sent as soon as possible. In a hurry to finish, Cameron noted that it was heavy by two swing-weights so milled two small dots, one on the putter head and one on the face heel which he then filled with cherry red marking. Three days later Tiger matched a career best 61 first round. This model was closely followed by an almost exact replica, but made from high-quality, German stainless steel and it was this one that went on to make history, winning many titles including 14 majors to date.

Long putters

I remember Sam Torrance turning up at a tournament with his long putter for the first time, in 1988. He had been struggling on the greens and his previously trusted, conventional stroke had got a little 'nervy'. Sam used his long putter with great success, as did Peter Senior, transforming his golf career. I experimented with a long putter and found that it was very effective from 6 feet in, but less so for longer putts.

There was no doubt that anchoring the putter to the body increased stability. As their use gained momentum the ruling bodies started to debate if the anchoring of putters gave an unfair advantage and whether the stroke was truly a swing. After much deliberation, the decision was made that as of 1 January 2016, anchoring while making a stroke was prohibited; players have to swing the entire club freely – just as they do with the others in their bag.

Bernhard Langer turned professional in 1972 and has battled a few putting difficulties along the way. In recent years, however, he has adapted his long putter technique with outstanding success. If you are struggling and haven't yet tried one, then give one a go.

According to the Rules of Golf, the length of the putter has no limit as long as it is a minimum of 18 inches.

Bernhard Langer uses a long putter, with great results.

In conclusion

In essence this chapter is about looking at the features that you need to take into consideration when choosing a putter. If there was one putter design that was so much better than any other, everybody would be using it. Picking the one that suits you personally gives the best chance to hole more putts.

chapter two

THE BASIC SET-UP

The right set-up is vital in giving you the foundation for a reliable and repeatable stroke.

GRIP FUNDAMENTALS

Now that you have chosen your putter it is time to move on to the the next rung of the ladder – the basics of the set-up and how to apply them.

These recommendations have been gleaned from my own experiences while studying the best putters and after hours of trial and error, experimenting and testing them. Let's start with your grip.

There are many ways of gripping the putter, but not all are equally effective at delivering the putter face squarely. Whatever grip you use, it should respect three basic fundamentals, as your hands on the grip are the only connection you have with the putter. They need to work in union, allowing you to control the putter face and feel how the ball has been struck. The fundamentals for a successful grip are: ensuring the palms face each other, avoiding any tension in the hands, and keeping the hands working together.

Palms facing

To demonstrate the first of these grip fundamentals just stand up and let your hands hang by your side. You will spot that your palms tend to hang facing each other. This is a natural position which you want to try and replicate when forming your grip.

Allow your hands and arms to hang naturally by your sides.

With your palms facing and positioned as though they are ready to clap, your hands are in the best position to deliver the putter face squarely.

Maintaining this natural position, move the arms forward with hands still facing.

Hands remain in the perfect position to make your grip.

Hand tension

Whatever grip you use, it is essential to avoid hand tension. Strangling the grip inhibits touch and the free swinging of the putter. The correct hand tension will allow you to:

- ○ Regulate the pace and rhythm of the stroke.
- ○ Retain touch and feel.
- ○ Help the putter head to swing.

If you are lacking in confidence you are more likely to grip too tightly.

Hands working together in unison

Whatever grip you use, you should not allow either hand to become too dominant during the stroke. It is very difficult to achieve consistency at impact without your hands working in harmony.

Egg test

Imagine you are holding two eggs. Grip them tight enough so as not to drop them but not so tightly that you break the shells. On a scale of 1–10, with 10 being as tight as you can squeeze and 1 being just tight enough that the putter doesn't slip out of your hand, you should be aiming for a 4–5 for the perfect tension. Tiger aims for a tension of 5.

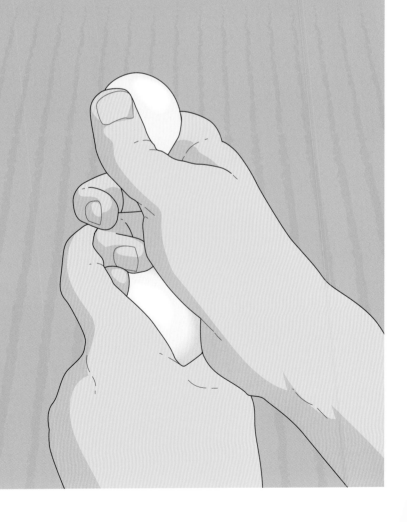

The benefits

Respecting my three basic grip fundamentals (palms facing, hand tension and hands working together in unison) will help you consistently:

○ Deliver the clubhead squarely.
○ Allow the sweet spot to strike the ball.
○ Judge the ball pace.
○ Swing the putter head rhythmically on the correct path.

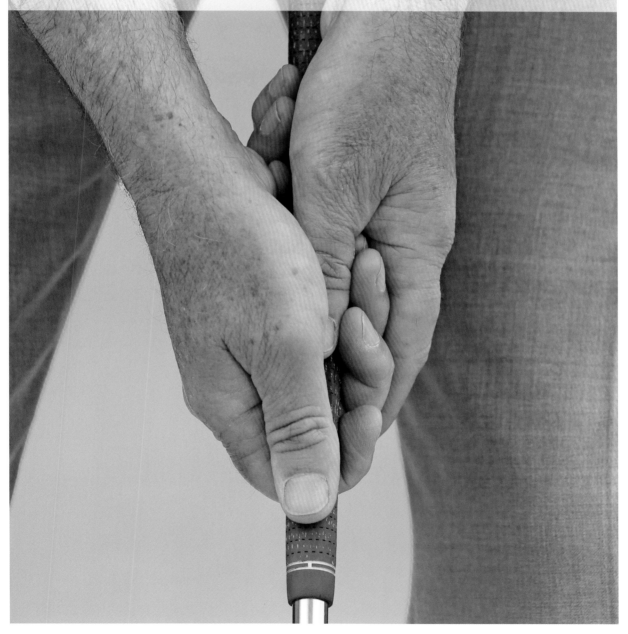

TAKING YOUR GRIP

The vast majority of the world's best players respect the three fundamentals of the grip.

Once you understand these fundamentals it is time to move on and try them out on your putter.

Follow these step-by-step instructions on how to position your hands and link them together to form your grip.

First, the left hand

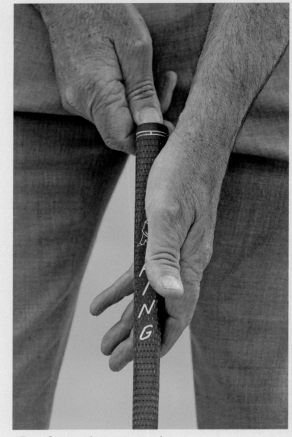

I Start with positioning the left hand, as shown here.

2 Then rest the grip on the pad of your hand, letting the putter fall over the middle joint of the index finger.

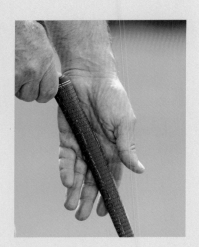

3 Form the grip with your thumb pointing downwards. The back of your hand should be facing down the aim line.

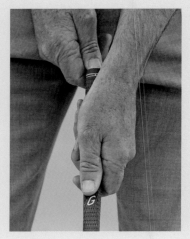

Now the right hand

1 *Let the grip sit comfortably against the pad of the hand, allowing it to run across the middle joint of the index finger with the thumb pointing down the front of the putter shaft.*

2 *The grip should be cradled between the right forefinger and the thumb.*

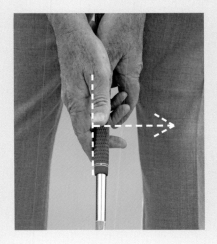

3 *Your palm should face along the intended aim line.*

Just like bowling, your palm should be facing the target as you release the ball.

Completing your grip

To finish off the grip, I suggest you use the reverse overlap method (see box, below). This grip uses the left forefinger to link the hands together, providing stability and unity. The combination of feel and union allows the putter to be held securely without unnecessary tension. Linking the hands together like this avoids one hand dominating the stroke.

Reverse overlap grip

○ With the left hand in place, raise the left index finger away from the grip.
○ Let the right hand slide up the grip to under the raised index finger, resting your little finger against the left middle finger.
○ Allow the left index finger to rest wherever most comfortable across the fingers of the right hand.

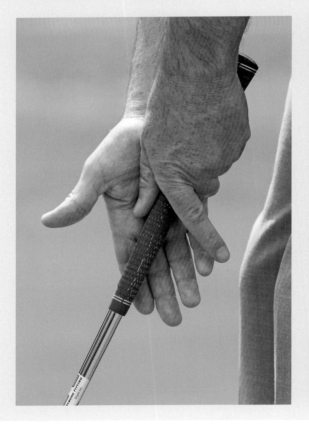

The completed grip

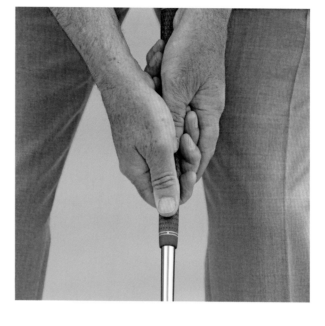

This uses the left forefinger to link the hands together, providing unity and stability.

The reverse overlap grip is favoured by many professionals including Jason Day, Brooks Koepka and Tiger Woods.

Who copied whom?

Checklist

○ Both thumbs run down the grip, helping to ensure the hands work as equal partners.

○ The shaft, left hand and forearm feel that they are blending comfortably together.

○ Palms are facing each other, the right palm at 90 degrees to your aim line.

Jason Day

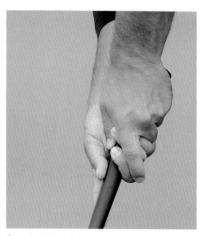

Brooks Koepka

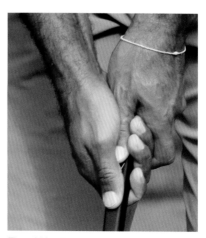

Tiger Woods

Other grips

Although the reverse overlap method is the one I suggest you try first, there are a number of other ways of gripping the putter. Here are some examples. Although they are all different, the vast majority adhere to the three basic fundamentals of palms facing, correct hand tension and hands working together. Never be afraid to try something new.

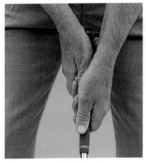

Cross-handed. Similar to the reverse overlap, but the left hand sits below the right.

The bunny grip. The shaft runs between the index and middle finger, forming a pair of bunny ears.

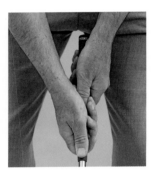

Two-handed. All fingers on the grip like those of a baseball player.

Pencil grip. The grip lies between your index finger and thumb, similar to holding a pencil.

Personal preference

Sergio Garcia's grip, although not conventional, still follows the three basic fundamentals.

To find out what type of grip Sergio used I thought it would be best to ask the question on Twitter. My query and his response are given below.

Ken Brown @KenBrownGolf 💬2hr
Does anyone know the difference between the 'claw' and the 'pencil' putting grips? ...What grip does @TheSergioGarcia use? Thanks

Sergio Garcia @TheSergioGarcia 💬1hr
@KenBrownGolf Claw: fingers are more on top of the grip. Pencil: fingers are more on the side of the grip. I prefer the pencil grip!

Sergio Garcia using the pencil grip.

CHRIS DIMARCO'S GRIP

In 2005, while commentating for BBC television at the Masters, Peter Alliss and I were watching Tiger and Chris DiMarco going head to head in the final round. That was the year Tiger landed his tee shot, on the par-three 16th, over the back of the green and played the most amazing chip, which toppled into the hole. If you haven't yet seen it, check it out on YouTube – you will not be disappointed. During that round I mentioned that Chris had a rather ungainly, unusual-looking grip, when compared to Tiger's textbook example, and asked Peter if he had ever seen anything like it before. He replied as quick as a flash: 'The first time I saw a grip like that was in the Gents at Paddington Station!' Cue a bout of uncontrollable laughter!

Having a grip that works effectively and efficiently is one of the most important factors to hole more putts. It may not always be conventional or beautiful.

'The claw took some of the right hand out of my stroke.'

ADDRESS

The most reliable and consistent way to deliver the club is to address the ball in the position you want to be in at impact. Start and finish in the same position.

The prime objective of the address is to provide a comfortable, stable base, one that minimizes core body movement. Setting up to the ball in the correct position is vital and relatively easy to do once you know how.

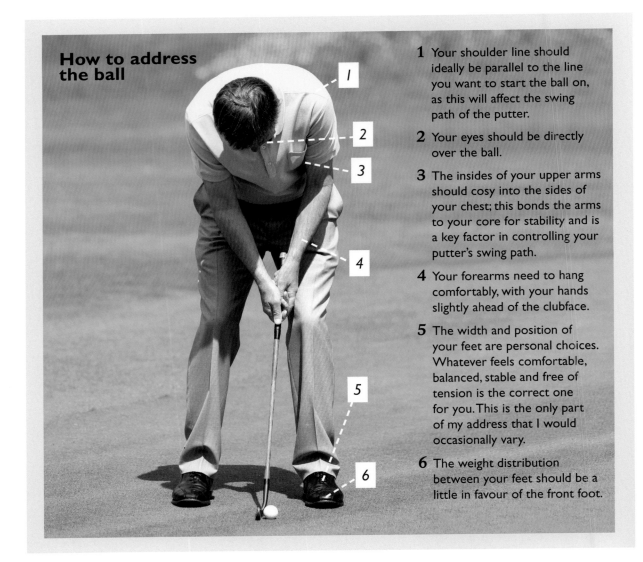

How to address the ball

1 Your shoulder line should ideally be parallel to the line you want to start the ball on, as this will affect the swing path of the putter.

2 Your eyes should be directly over the ball.

3 The insides of your upper arms should cosy into the sides of your chest; this bonds the arms to your core for stability and is a key factor in controlling your putter's swing path.

4 Your forearms need to hang comfortably, with your hands slightly ahead of the clubface.

5 The width and position of your feet are personal choices. Whatever feels comfortable, balanced, stable and free of tension is the correct one for you. This is the only part of my address that I would occasionally vary.

6 The weight distribution between your feet should be a little in favour of the front foot.

Spot the difference

Address

Impact

Address

The ball position should be at the bottom of the swing arc, the lowest point in the stroke where the sole of the club grazes the grass. This will vary from just inside the left foot to a few inches further back depending on the stance width.

Impact

The putter returns to the position you have addressed the ball in. The most efficient and simplest way to deliver the club is achieved by starting and finishing in the same place; it eliminates the need for any manipulations during your stroke.

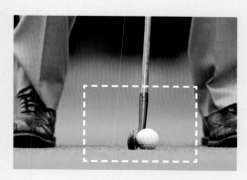

Address

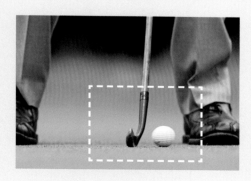

Impact

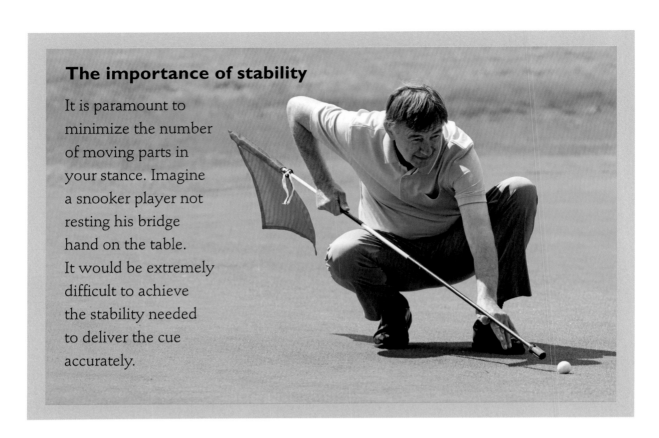

The importance of stability

It is paramount to minimize the number of moving parts in your stance. Imagine a snooker player not resting his bridge hand on the table. It would be extremely difficult to achieve the stability needed to deliver the cue accurately.

You will be amazed how keeping still will improve your putting. You can only be ready when you are steady.

Eyes over the ball

Another helpful factor that will greatly enhance your ability to hole putts consistently, especially from within 8 feet, is getting your eyes directly over the ball at address. If you watch the best snooker players, they look directly down the cue to the white ball. If they moved their head it would become a real challenge to make a precise contact and start the ball on the chosen line; the same applies to putting.

Checking your eyes are over the ball

Having your eyes over the ball with your eyes parallel to the aim line will help with your alignment. Start by addressing the ball, then:

1 Hold another ball on the bridge of your nose.
2 Drop it.
3 The dropped ball should make a direct hit with the one you are addressing.

THE SET-UPS OF SIX PROS

One of the best ways to achieve a perfect set-up is to learn from the best. Let's look at how six leading pros set up, what you can learn and what they have in common.

RICKIE FOWLER

I first saw Rickie Fowler play at the Walker Cup at Royal County Down in 2007. He was 18, but looked 14, and it was already evident that he was hugely gifted and natural. A very popular player and an inspiration to the next generation of golfers.

○ Feet, knees and shoulders run parallel to the aim line, all look soft yet stable ... Perfect.
○ Classic overlap grip, fingers close together, helping his hands to work as a unit.
○ Ball addressed on the sweet spot.
○ Putter set-up has been personalized so that the lie and length allow his arms to hang naturally, with eyes over the ball.
○ Everything looks simple and natural.

RORY MCILROY

Northern Ireland's best golfer with four Major titles by the age of 25. I first interviewed Rory when he was 14 and a few years later partnered him on his first hole as a professional at the Belfry. What fun it has been for all of us to watch his amazing success.

❍ Neutral reverse overlap grip.

❍ The back of the left hand facing down his line.

❍ Upper arms connected to his chest.

❍ Shoulders parallel to his aim line, helping the putter swing on the correct path.

❍ Works hard on his set-up routine, making it simple and unhurried.

❍ Upper arms snuggle into body.

It is interesting to see such varying set-up styles – from the classic Luke Donald one to Michelle Wie's table-top set-up. However when you look closely, all six pros adhere to the three fundamentals of the grip (see page 52), take a stable stance with eyes over the ball and address the ball in the position they would like to return to at impact. This provides the foundation to develop an efficient repeatable stroke.

LUKE DONALD

One of the best in the business, Luke proves the theory that 'simplicity is profound' when it comes to putting.

❍ Set-up looks balanced and tension free.

❍ Perfect grip: hands blend together, and his thumbs point down to the putter head.

❍ No sign of tension in the hands, arms or shoulders.

❍ Luke's upper arms just blend into the body, giving them stability.

❍ Weighting slightly favours his left side.

❍ Ball is addressed from the sweet spot.

❍ Luke always sets himself goals when practising his putts.

❍ He achieves just the right pace to give the ball the best chance of finding the hole.

MICHELLE WIE

I first saw Michelle play when, aged 14, she came over to Formby with the US Curtis Cup team. As a 6-foot (1.8-metre) 14-year-old, she was without doubt the most impressive youngster I had ever seen. It took her a little while to settle into the Tour scene, but in 2014 she took her first Major, the US Women's Open. A turning point in her putting came when watching Ai Miyazato putt who, at 5 foot (1.5 metres) tall in her stilettos, made Michelle think 'I'm too far from the ball'. She subsequently adopted this technique and reaped the benefits! Just like Michelle, many pros experiment with and change their technique to find what works best for them.

❍ Upper arms now snuggle cosily in.
❍ Eyes over the ball help her to see the line better.
❍ Cross-handed grip, the left hand below the right with the palms facing each other.
❍ Shoulder aligned down her aim line.
❍ Address position that helps Michelle eliminate any body movement throughout her stroke.

PHIL MICKELSON

Winner of more than 40 events on the PGA Tour, including the Open, the US PGA and the Masters. His touch on and around the greens is up there with the best that have ever played.

❍ The putter is set up perfectly, length, lie and loft. Phil's address position looks very comfortable.

❍ Balanced stance.

❍ No tension in the grip, helping maintain an unhurried rhythm which is so important on fast greens.

❍ Visualizing his putt as he looks down the aim line.

❍ You always get the feeling that the putter head swings in Phil's hands.

❍ Take a snap on your camera to check out your address position.

TIGER WOODS

Looks like he was born to putt. His dad taught him golf from 'the hole out', perhaps that's why. Textbook address – if you want someone to copy Tiger Woods is your man.

❍ Always looks rock steady, yet free of any tension.
❍ Perfectly balanced.
❍ Putter and posture fit together like a jigsaw.
❍ Eyes over the ball and parallel to his aim line.
❍ Beautiful reverse overlap grip.
❍ Mindful of his grip pressure.
❍ A perfect address leads to a perfect stroke.

Now you have a putter that suits you and have gained an understanding of the basic set-up, you have given yourself the optimum chance to deliver the club correctly and consistently.

Before you actually make a stroke, let's now take a look at how you decide in which direction and at what speed you need to hit the ball in order to make a One Putt.

chapter three

READING
GREENS

Reading greens is an essential
component of holing one putts.

APPROACHING THE GREEN

Even with the best putting stroke in the world you will not hole your share of putts unless you can read the greens. This is your chance to be Sherlock Holmes. Like a detective, you need to be observant, use your experience and a certain amount of intuition.

Let's begin the search for clues by studying how your ball reacts as it lands on the green. This gives you an indication of the green's texture and contours by seeing how high and what direction the ball bounces.

Walking towards your ball, note the colour and feel of the putting surface. Is it verdant green, sun parched, firm or soft? All could be pointers as to the pace of the green. Don't assume that the greener the surface the slower the pace; some of the modern cultivars of grass can be emerald-green and still very fast – just like those at Augusta National.

As you walk onto the green your putting routine begins. This should be calm and methodical – rushing around will often result in a rushed stroke. Next time you watch the top pros you will notice that their routine is a well-choreographed dance – more a waltz than a jive – and is the same every time. Every putt is unique. You are always starting from scratch.

Take a tip from the surrounding terrain which can provide clues as to how the green slopes.

Any sand splashed onto the the green results in a faster, firmer area.

How far did your ball bounce when it landed? This gives another clue as to the speed of the green.

What to look out for when you walk onto the green

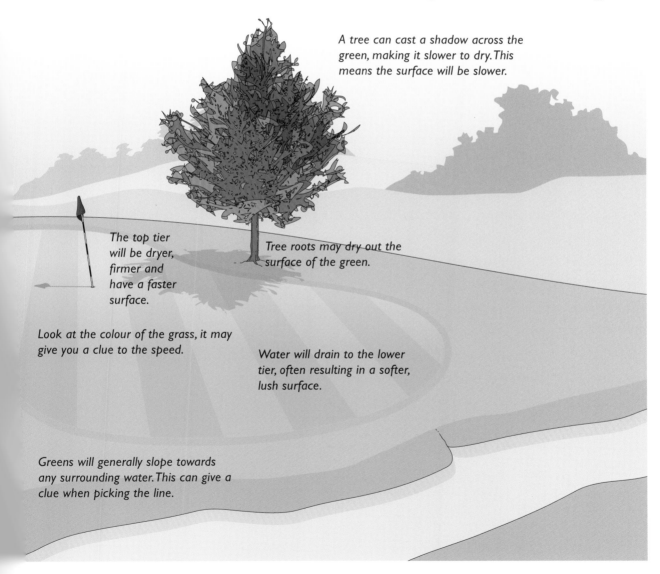

A tree can cast a shadow across the green, making it slower to dry. This means the surface will be slower.

The top tier will be dryer, firmer and have a faster surface.

Tree roots may dry out the surface of the green.

Look at the colour of the grass, it may give you a clue to the speed.

Water will drain to the lower tier, often resulting in a softer, lush surface.

Greens will generally slope towards any surrounding water. This can give a clue when picking the line.

MENDING THE PITCH MARK

When you repair your, and possibly other, pitch marks feel how the pitch fork goes into the green. This will help to confirm what you have felt underfoot and guide you in determining the texture and speed of the green.

Pitch marks should be repaired by teasing the area all round the indentation, gently moving the turf back to its original spot. If you insert the pitch fork into just one place a bare patch will be left in the centre. When done correctly, a pitch mark will recover in 48 hours; when done incorrectly, it may take up to three weeks to disappear. Once repaired, the surface should be tapped down with the sole of the putter.

Marking the ball

I recommend a traditional ball-marker with a spike underneath to help secure its position and give you another opportunity to note how the turf yields. You may remember what happened to Ian Poulter in 2010 during a play-off against Robert Karlsson in Dubai. He accidentally dropped the ball on his marker, causing it to move and so received a one-stroke penalty, costing him a chance of victory in the World Tour Championship with a first prize of £750,000. Incidents such as this led to a rule change, so now there is no penalty if a player's ball or ball-marker on the putting green are accidentally moved.

Cleaning and checking your ball

You now have the chance to inspect the ball for battle scars and clean away any trace of moisture, mud or grass which may affect its roll.

Markers

○ A large marker will be easier to see when you are lining up longer putts.

○ Some pros carry two markers: one large and one small.

○ Your marker should preferably be a small, round, flat object but could be anything of your choice.

○ It is recommended to place your marker as close as possible directly behind the ball.

BROOKLINE 1999

Mark James kindly invited me to be one of his vice captains for the 1999 Ryder Cup in Brookline. There were lots of tales to tell from that week's golf but this is one that didn't make the headlines.

One of my tasks for the Sunday singles was to stand on the par-three 2nd to relay information to Mark on the club selection of previous groups. Jarmo Sandelin (above) was third match out, making his first Ryder Cup appearance and drawn against Phil Mickelson. He played up to the green, putted out and then I saw him waving furiously in my direction. I raced up in a bit of a panic to be told that he had lost his favourite marker. It was a Swedish coin for which he had no replacement.

You can become very attached to a 'lucky' marker, and for this to have happened in such a high-pressure situation would only have exacerbated Jarmo's Ryder Cup nerves.

I needed to focus on the next group on the tee so I caught the attention of my wife and tasked her with finding a replacement. She walked among the crowd asking anybody who looked remotely Scandinavian if they had a Swedish coin. By the 4th tee a suitable krona had been found and passed over to Jarmo.

Just like a highly tuned Formula 1 car, if there is any little component out of place the effect can be disproportionately unbalancing.

LET THE READING BEGIN

This is not an easy task to put into words, but I will try and describe some ways to figure out what the break and pace of a putt are going to be.

To start assessing the green, I squat 2–3 yards behind the ball, looking down the line; this gives me a good view of the whole putt. Some players find it easier to be slightly nearer or further from the ball, and some golfers remain standing.

By always using the same viewing position, with your eyes in the same spot, you gain a consistent perspective, thereby enabling you to draw from past experience.

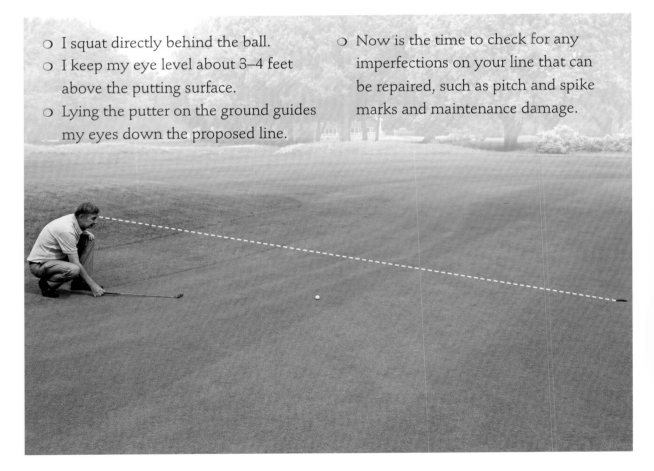

○ I squat directly behind the ball.
○ I keep my eye level about 3–4 feet above the putting surface.
○ Lying the putter on the ground guides my eyes down the proposed line.

○ Now is the time to check for any imperfections on your line that can be repaired, such as pitch and spike marks and maintenance damage.

What the pros do

Georgia Hall, Rory McIlroy, Seve and Brooks Koepka all adopt a similar position when reading the greens, which is the one most commonly used by Tour players. Squatting to a height where your eye level is roughly in line with the top of your grip will give you a good perspective of the line and help you adopt a consistent position like Seve.

Top left and right: Georgia and Rory study their lines. Bottom left: Brooks reads the green. Bottom right: the master craftsman in the perfect position.

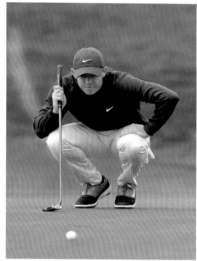

IF YOU ARE UNSURE …

You might find it helpful to look from different angles if you are not certain of the line or just need further confirmation.

If you need a second look, don't take too long and keep up with the speed of play. Walk in a circle around the ball and hole, checking the different viewpoints and letting the putter swing freely in your hand as you do so. This will give you a feel of the putter and help keep any hand tension at bay. Jack Nicklaus used to do this with his right hand, Dave Stockton with his left – both were great putters.

1 Look from behind your ball to get an idea of the line.

2 Circle the whole putt starting on the low side.

3 Gather more information on the line from directly behind the hole.

4 Three quarters of the way round look to see if the putt is uphill or downhill.

Different views?

These two photographs show the same piece of card held in the same position but viewed from two different angles. The image on the right shows the line of the putt from behind, making it a little easier to identify the break. From this perspective you can see that the hole edge tilts from right to left, meaning that the putt will also break from right to left break.

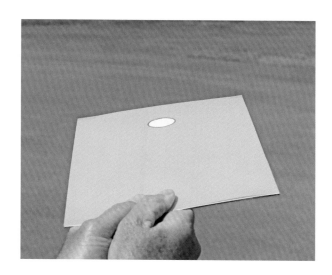

But is it uphill or downhill?

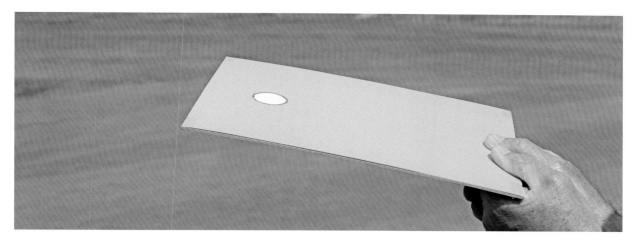

Viewing from the side will often give you a better clue of the gradient. The left of the hole is higher than the right, indicating an uphill putt.

It is harder to see the break from a side view. Looking towards the cup, depending on how much of the white inside is visible, you can get an idea of the direction in which the green is sloping around the hole.

Don't forget that as the ball reaches the hole any breaks will be accentuated as it slows in pace, so just give the last yard a little extra attention.

Marking your ball may help

You must be able to identify your ball when playing in competition, and some players use a marker pen to do this. Any identity marks can also help with alignment.

I was one of the first players to utilize this alignment mark to help with my aim. It gave me a focal point, which kept my

head still and helped square the putter face. It was something I did all my career.

This is the most popular way to mark the ball on Tour and is used by many tournament pros. They point the line towards where they want the ball to start rolling. As a professional, I spent my working life trying to eke out any slight advantage, any little thing that put the percentage in my favour. On the right, you see Tiger Woods doing just this as he points the mark on his ball down his aim line. Try it to help with your aim and alignment.

Flag in, flag out

You can have the flagstick in, out or attended; the choice is yours.

If your ball is destined for the hole, that is where it will end up, regardless of whether the flagstick is in or out, so what are the advantages of having it in? Firstly, if you hit the ball too hard an in-situ flagstick will either allow the ball to drop in or slow it down, giving you a shorter putt next. Secondly, it will help to visualize the target and is a nice reference for longer putts.

Bryson DeChambeau
believes it's an advantage
to keep the flag in.

Returning to your starting position

You can now put together all of your observations and make a final decision on the exact aim line. With confidence, I say in my head what needs to happen: 'One inch outside the left and a little uphill'.

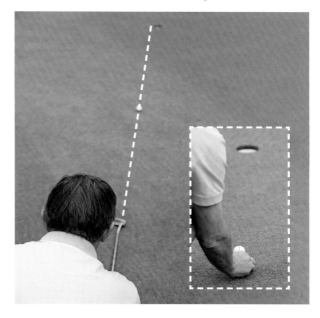

If those who played before you left the flagstick leaning you can leave it as is or move it to a centred position. Flagsticks vary in rigidity; the less rigid are more forgiving.

If I was playing a casual round, the flag would never leave the hole, but for competition golf I would take into account the length, difficulty and how confident I felt of hitting the ball at the correct speed before deciding; as a rule of thumb for anything over 15 feet the flagstick would remain in.

❍ It is helpful to point the putter shaft down the aim line.
❍ Line up the logo or other ball marking down the same line.
❍ Visualize the putt, how it starts on the aim line and rolls into the cup.

Now you know the line, you are ready to take the next step up the ladder, but before you do, the following pages contain a few other pointers to help you read greens.

YARDAGE BOOKS

From about the age of 14 I have kept guides or yardage books of every course I have played or worked on as a TV commentator. How can this help in reading greens?

You will often see Tour pros gazing at their yardage books on the greens. They are looking at their notes taken during a practice round or from a previous year's tournament. Your notes should affirm what you see, and this will give you an edge of confidence that you have chosen the right line.

My pal Mark James used to say that if I had appeared on *University Challenge* it would have been 'Hi, I'm Ken Brown, I'm from Harpenden and I'm reading Greens.'

This is just a sample of some yardage books that I have accumulated over the years.

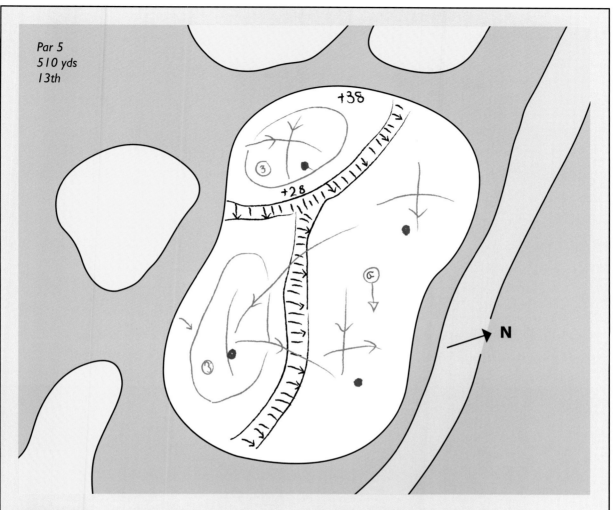

Par 5
510 yds
13th

+38

+28

N

Annotating a yardage book

During practice rounds I look where the potential hole positions might be. If there is nobody behind me, I hit a couple of putts from different angles and make notes on the breaks in the yardage book. This example shows my notes from the 13th green at Augusta National:

○ The blue dots mark the four pin positions used on each day of the tournament.

○ The lines and arrows indicate the breaks and direction of the slopes.

○ 'G' is the general direction of the grain on the grass.

○ I have a simple code from 1–3 that gives a guide to the severity of the slope. A 1 slope is impossible to stop the ball from above the cup, while a 3 slope is fairly flat.

THE CUT LINES

The 'cut lines' on the green are the stripes created by the mower roller when cutting the grass. The blades of grass are flattened in the direction the mower has travelled.

This can affect the pace and line of a putt. Putting directly down the lighter cut line, where the grain on the grass is running away from you, will cause the ball to run faster. Putting into the dark line, where the grain is leaning towards you, the ball will run slower.

The cut lines will have virtually no effect on well-maintained summer greens.

However early spring greens and those cut with a wide sit-on mower are more likely to affect the ball. Putting across cut lines will cause the ball to weave as it crosses the grain; this is called 'snaking'.

It is much harder to predict the effect of any grain for putts of more than 10 feet as the ball is likely to be crossing several cut lines.

The grass blades on the shiny lighter line will be leaning away from you.

Bermuda greens

Bermuda grasses are commonly used in hot climates because they are resilient to higher temperatures. These grasses, which originally came from Africa, have thick, coarse blades, but modern cultivars have been developed to create a smooth and durable putting surface.

Bermuda greens generally have more grain. It is quite easy to see which way it's going. When the grass is looking its shiniest, it is growing away from you, so will be a faster putt. Conversely when it looks its darkest, it is growing directly towards you and will be slower. When putting across the grain the ball will turn further than the slope suggests. Reading the strength and direction of the grain on a Bermuda green adds another element to picking the line.

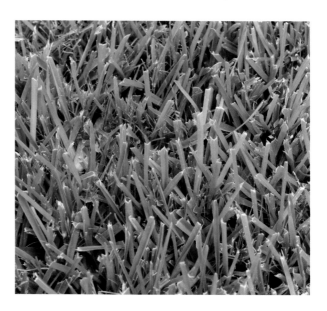

Here is how the grain affects the cup

- ○ Looking into this cup you can see the edge of the hole has broken down.
- ○ The grass is growing away from the broken edge.
- ○ Because the roots were severed when the hole was cut, the grass gradually died as the day went by, causing the hole edge to break up. The stronger the grain the more the cup edge gives way.
- ○ This only gives you the direction of the grain around the hole.

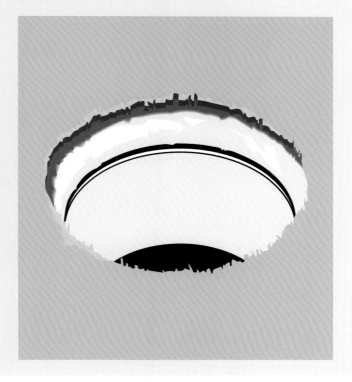

CAN YOU KEEP A SECRET?

When it comes to turning the odds in your favour, take a tip from Nick Faldo, captain of the 2008 Ryder Cup team.

Before the singles he sent out his vice captain, José María Olazábal, and top caddy, Billy Foster, to check the pin positions and note the best area to hit the approach shots and leave the easiest putts. They also marked areas of each green that should be avoided and any other helpful tips to be given to each team member. Billy Foster gave me the original, telling me not to show it to anybody. I've kept the secret until now!

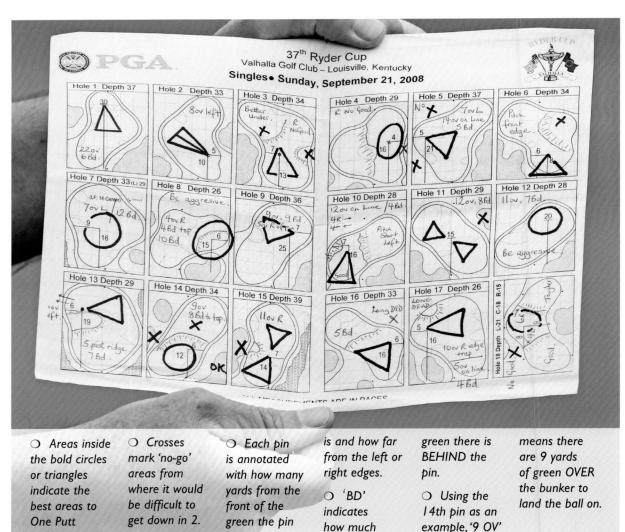

○ Areas inside the bold circles or triangles indicate the best areas to One Putt

○ Crosses mark 'no-go' areas from where it would be difficult to get down in 2.

○ Each pin is annotated with how many yards from the front of the green the pin is and how far from the left or right edges.

○ 'BD' indicates how much green there is BEHIND the pin.

○ Using the 14th pin as an example, '9 OV' means there are 9 yards of green OVER the bunker to land the ball on.

GREEN-READING GLASSES

During the 2004 World Matchplay at Wentworth Seve joined the BBC commentary team. A veteran of the event, he had lots to offer the viewers. For the final on the Sunday he joined me and the crew; with only one match to follow there was ample opportunity to liven things up. The final was between Ernie Els and Lee Westwood, and if Ernie came out on top he would beat the record held jointly by Seve and Gary Player of five World Matchplay titles.

What a day it turned out to be. Seve was friends with both Lee and Ernie, and I think having him on the fairway added to their excitement. Back in 1994 Ernie and Seve had battled away in an epic World Matchplay duel until victory for Ernie – a match Ernie still talks about to this day.

We filmed a few bits to camera as the day went on and Seve was loving every minute, chatting to the gallery, hugging the grannies and the children, signing anything that a pen would mark and posing for photos. It was a pleasure to witness the affection the fans had for Seve. It was a day when the golf almost seemed secondary to the gallery's appreciation for the BBC's new commentator.

Before we went out, Nick – one of the cameramen – had lent me a pair of 'green-reading glasses', a purchase from his local joke shop. I asked if I could borrow them as they might come in handy. He smiled generously and passed them over. When we reached the 11th green I quizzed Seve if he could still read greens as well as he used to. While everything was going out live, I suggested he try some recently launched green-reading glasses. Without hesitation he said 'Yes, that would be great.' He took them and put them on. We both dissolved laughing, as did the crowd. Later Ernie triumphed for a record sixth win – a joyous scene indeed.

There are lots of gizmos and technology around to help improve your golf, but genuine green-reading glasses are yet to be invented.

chapter four

THE SET-UP ROUTINE

The best way to handle pressure is to establish a pre-shot routine.

REHEARSE YOUR ROUTINE

In my early years as a pro the late Sir Henry Cotton, three-time Open winner, invited me to stay with him at Penina, Portugal for winter practice. One of the pearls of wisdom he bestowed on me was the importance of a set-up routine. It took me the full four weeks of my first stay to develop and practise it.

The one I describe here works for me but there are many variations. You need to find something that helps you set up in the same position every time and is easily repeated. Whatever you decide should become second nature – this is not the time for pondering. A good set-up routine becomes a subconscious comforter and the backbone to hole more putts under pressure.

Here we go!

As you step up to the ball resist any inclination to rush. Your whole routine should be fluid, smooth and nicely oiled.

A change in tempo now will be transferred into a more hurried rhythm in your stroke.

Practice strokes

○ Set yourself up close to the ball. South African golf legend Denis Hutchinson says: 'All the best putters seem to snuggle in behind the ball.'
○ The practice stroke is a dry run – it should emulate the one you are about to make.
○ Keep your grip tender and light.
○ Let the sole of the putter lightly brush the surface of the grass.
○ I recommend 1–2 practice strokes.

If you have second thoughts at any stage or something breaks your concentration, step away and start again.

The final step

○ Step up to the ball.
○ With a couple of looks, align the putter face along the aim line, with the ball in front of the sweet spot.
○ Remember your hand tension should be as though you are cradling an egg.
○ You are now in an ideal position to make your stroke.

RORY'S HARD LESSON

'I learnt so much more from my Sunday collapse at Augusta National than I did from the whole experience of winning the US Open.' Honest words from a supremely talented young golfer.

Going into the final round of the Masters in 2011 Rory McIlroy was ahead by four strokes, a slender lead for such a testing course, but he still had the opportunity to win his first green jacket. As part of my work for the BBC I did a little analysis of Rory's putting routine so it could be broadcast before he set off from the 1st tee that afternoon. Using a split screen I compared two of his putts from the Saturday. Playing the pictures simultaneously, it was incredible to see that the timing, his movements and every little gesture were identical. The question was could he replicate this under such intense pressure?

Sadly, circumstances caused the routine to get rushed in his final round and Rory signed for an 80. As he headed for the scorer's hut with that 'get me out of here, lost boy' look there could not have been a viewer who didn't want to hug him and tell him that his day would come. It was a devastating experience, yet Rory went on to win the US Open that year. He reflected: 'Everyone makes mistakes, so it is all about taking what you can from them. There is no point in dwelling on the past because you can't change that. You can definitely change what happens in the future.'

Watch his putting routine next time you see him; it is simple, brisk, no nonsense – always the same and never rushed.

A day to forget, but one he will always remember.

THE SUPREME ROUTINE

Never will a pro experience more pressure than at the Ryder Cup, when he is playing for himself, Europe and his team mates. In the Medinah 2012 matches Martin Kaymer was faced with the ultimate pressure putt to keep the dream alive in his Sunday singles match; it was not unlike the crucial one missed by his fellow German, Bernhard Langer, at Kiawah Island in 1991. Afterwards Martin was asked if he had thought of Bernhard's putt.

'I don't like the question but, yes, it's true. I did think about him. Especially when I walked around the other side and there was a footprint on my line. But it was not that bad, so I thought it's ok, it's not going to happen again. I didn't really think about missing. There was only one choice, you have to make it. I was not nervous, I was so very controlled because I knew exactly what I had to do. But if you ask me how the putt went in, I have no idea. I can't remember. When it went in, I was just very happy.'

A day he will always remember and never forget.

The set-up routine is very personal. Watch the pros and choose one that looks simple and easy to repeat.

chapter five

THE STROKE

Let's get the ball rolling
on your chosen line.

THE FINAL FRONTIER

Everything we have looked at so far has prepared you for the final frontier – to make a stroke that will start the ball down your chosen aim line at the right speed.

When watching the amazing talent of any great sportsman or woman, what you will witness is the culmination of years of dedicated preparation. Take one of snooker's finest players, Ronnie O'Sullivan, as an example. In 1997 he scored the fastest maximum break – 147 in 5 minutes and 20 seconds – potting 36 balls. What seemed utterly effortless was in fact a combination of prodigious talent and a practice regime based on the 'snooker ladder'.

As we climb the putting ladder, it is helpful to have an understanding of the factors that will affect the ball's direction and speed. These are the putter face angle, the swing path, the angle of attack and striking the ball from the sweet spot.

1 Putter face angle

The angle between the putter face and the aim line is the factor that has the biggest influence on the ball's direction. Ideally the putter face should be pointing squarely down the aim line at impact. If it is open, the ball will start to the right, and if the face is closed it will veer to the left.

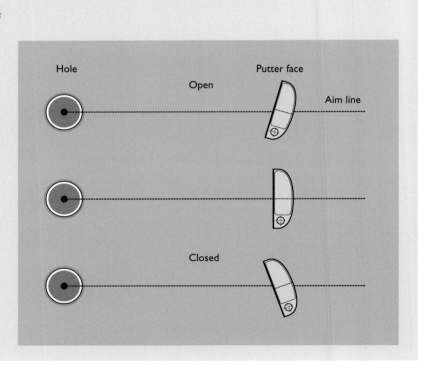

Everyone's swing path is slightly different, depending on their height, how far they stand from the ball and their address.

Who can resist a flicker sequence? Get flicking!

2 Swing path

This is the direction the putter is swung in relation to the aim line. The swing path will influence the ball's direction at impact, but less so than the face angle. Keeping the inside of your upper arms lightly in contact with the sides of your chest will naturally help regulate the putter's path.

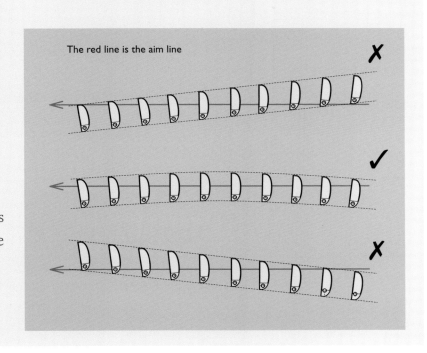

The red line is the aim line

✗

✓

✗

Address

Back

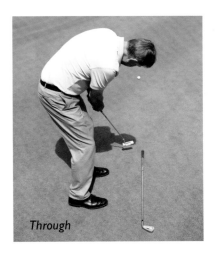

Through

3 Angle of attack

This is the angle of the putter head on the downswing. Below illustrates both steep and shallow angles of attack and describes the effects they each have on the ball.

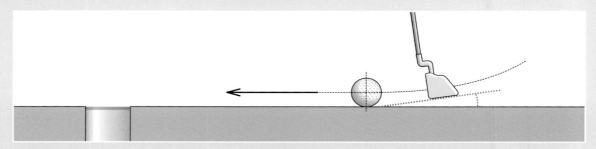

Steep angle
Hitting down on the ball with a steep angle of attack often starts the ball bouncing off the putter face, making it more difficult to judge the speed and line of the shot.

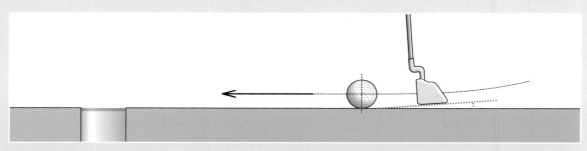

Shallow angle
A shallow angle of attack allows the putter head to hug the grass through impact, which is the most effective way to return the putter face squarely and get the ball rolling in a controlled way.

Keeping the putter low to the grass through impact helps get the ball rolling.

4 The importance of hitting the sweet spot

The sweet spot is the point on the putter where the face is stable at impact. If the ball is struck anywhere else, the face will twist, affecting how far the ball rolls and its direction. The further away from the sweet spot the ball is struck, the more the face twists and less energy is imparted, losing control of pace and line.

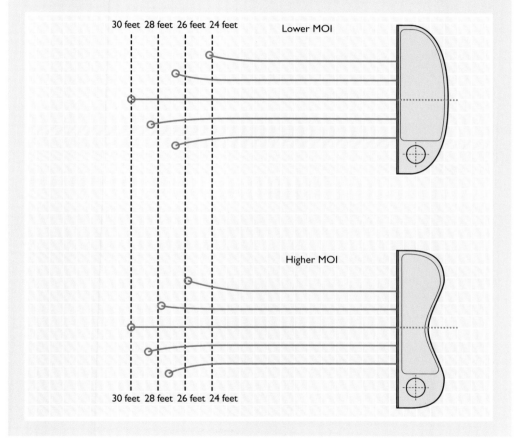

Both of these putters are identical weights. When used to hit a 30-foot putt, the distance the ball travels will vary depending on which part of the face strikes the ball. When hitting from the sweet spot the energy from both putters is identical. If you miss the sweet spot the one with higher MOI results in less variation in how far the ball travels.

Three balls hit, only one from the sweet spot.

The result!

FITTING IT TOGETHER

Now that you are armed with the knowledge of what affects the ball's direction and speed, let's start by addressing the ball. Simple!

The ball should be positioned at the bottom of the putter's swing arc. This is the lowest point in the stroke, where the sole of the putter grazes the grass. When addressing the ball, the back of the left hand should be very slightly ahead of the ball, giving the feeling of the shaft, the left hand and forearm working as a team.

Addressing the ball

1 The sweet spot is facing the back of the ball.

2 Eyes should be directly over the ball.

3 Hands are bonded as a unit, keeping the grip light and free of tension.

4 Trust is a must! Don't ponder over the ball too long!

The goal is simple: bring the putter face square along the intended line at the correct pace.

Backswing

1 Keep all moving parts to a minimum, and your head absolutely steady.

2 Ensure the shaft and the left wrist are still in virtually the same position as they were at address.

3 Make sure the grip is light and constant.

4 Snuggle the upper arms close to the chest for stability and to stop them swinging independently.

5 Swing the putter head using mainly the arms; the wrists will hinge in response to the weight of the head and no more.

Impact

1 Putter has returned to the address position with the shaft, left hand and forearm still in line.

2 Ball has just been struck from the sweet spot.

3 Eyes remain fixed on the ball.

4 Grip pressure remains constant.

5 Hands are still marginally leading the clubhead.

Putter head trajectory

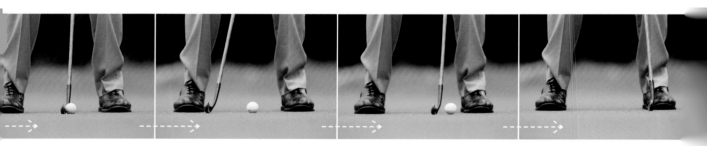

These close-up views show how low the head stays to the ground through the hitting area. This really helps in returning the putter to your address position and has the benefits of being the correct angle of attack, finding the sweet spot and regulating your swing path. It is the most reliable way to impart optimum roll on the ball.

No peeking

1 Body remains still, stability increases reliability.

2 The putter head continues to swing while remaining low to the ground.

3 To maintain balance make sure the weight distribution between your feet remains the same as it was at address.

Follow-through

1 The head is just starting to rotate, but the body remains steady.

2 The weight of the swinging putter head has caused the left wrist to release naturally.

3 Upper arms have not ventured away from the body.

A COUPLE OF USEFUL TIPS

Let the putter head swing

This implies a free rhythmical motion, with the clubhead swinging from the momentum of its own weight. How does swing help your stroke? It:

- Enhances flow and tempo.
- Regulates the stroke length.
- Makes it easier to hit the sweet spot reliably.
- Gives you touch.

You can't teach swing – you have to feel it. Here is a simple drill that will give you the sensation of the club swinging.

1 Hold the putter at the end of the grip between your finger and thumb and start it swinging back and forth with the other hand. Notice three things: how lightly you are holding the club, the tick-tock rhythm and the path the head is swinging on.

2 Next grip your putter lightly with just one hand and make some one-handed strokes. Try to get the feel of the club swinging in the same way as it had done in step 1.

3 Keeping the feel of the swing and only that, add the other hand and hit some 10-foot putts.

The better you get that feel of the club swinging, the more it will enrich the other aspects of your stroke.

I'll leave you in Tiger's hands...

As Tiger makes his stroke, the club sits lightly in his fingers, allowing the putter to 'swing' rhythmically and his hands to work perfectly together. I cannot over-emphasize the importance of maintaining a light grip; grasping the club tightly makes 'the swing' impossible.

Tap in the tack

This is a good way to visualize and help you understand the most effective and efficient way to strike the ball consistently.

Imagine the head of a small tack sticking out of the ball's equator. This is the point on which you need to make contact with your putter. The flat head of the tack is set at right angles to your aim line.

Question: How do you drive the tack into the ball most effectively?

Answer: By hitting the tack squarely from the sweet spot with the putter travelling down the aim line.

Nail it!

Imagine the putter is a hammer

If you mishit the tack, at best it goes in crookedly and at worst you end up with a throbbing thumb. Mishitting a putt will be just as penalizing.

Luke Donald's stroke, one of the best!

When you put all the fundamentals together this is how it should look; there is no better example than Luke Donald's ONE PUTT!

chapter six

TOUCH AND FEEL

Build your touch, feel and confidence with these simple drills.

8 ONE PUTTING!

7 TIPS AND DRILLS

6 TOUCH AND FEEL

5 THE STROKE

4 THE SET-UP ROUTINE

3 READING GREENS

2 THE BASIC SET-UP

1 CHOOSING A PUTTER

CAUSE AND EFFECT

It's time now to move on from the mechanics of the dance and focus on the rhythm of the music. This step up the ladder will develop your touch and feel.

With sound mechanics it is much easier to improve your touch and feel. Indeed you could also say that with a good touch it is easier to have sound mechanics. The importance of touch and feel is often overlooked when searching for technical mastery; they need to work in partnership like Fred Astaire and Ginger Rogers.

Three players who come quickly to mind when you think of outstanding touch and feel are Inbee Park, Rickie Fowler and Jordan Spieth; they all seem to possess a supernatural touch. The reality is they have consistent, reliable strokes and they put time in on the practice green.

Another master was Isao Aoki. I can remember one morning in Portmarnock before he and I teed off in the 1981 Irish Open. Aoki, who was Japan's top golfer at the time, dropped three balls on the practice green firstly holing them from 3 feet, then 5 feet, then 6 feet, then 12 feet and finally 30 feet … all dropping into the centre of the cup! He looked up, smiled and said in his broken English: 'I'm ready'.

Touch cannot be taught – it can only be acquired.

Touch and feel are developed from the ability to recognize what action caused what result and then being able to adapt that action to fit the next intended result. There are no short cuts but the following simple drills will make the necessary practice more enjoyable and fruitful and so help you ONE PUTT.

TWO-PUTT DRILL

This is a practice drill that I have used since a lad, one that takes on all the departments of putting and really helps develop touch.

You need three balls of the same type, preferably new ones. Set up eight starting points, evenly spaced, around the perimeter of the green, marking each with a tee. Hit three balls from each spot, trying to complete the eight-'hole' course in as few putts as possible. If you allow yourself two putts per ball this would give an overall par of 48. Breaking this is not easy, even on a small green. With just a small improvement in your lag putting you will start to eliminate some of those three putts.

○ By using three balls from each tee you can modify line or pace if you make a misjudgement, building your feel.

○ Keeping a score adds an element of competition and allows you to track your improvement.

○ You are practising touch and feel from various lengths.

○ Remember to keep your head steady – you will then find the sweet spot (see page 26) more often.

Develop touch and you will see more one and two putts, never three!

ONE-HANDED PUTTING

Putting with one hand is an excellent routine with a number of benefits. It's also Tiger's favourite drill.

1 You can use either hand, whichever feels most comfortable.

2 Using just one hand makes the putter feel heavier than usual, giving you a real sense of rhythm.

3 It lets the hand release naturally without being too wristy.

4 It helps regulate the length of your stroke.

5 It helps keep your upper arm in contact with your body which will greatly increase your chance of delivering the sweet spot to the ball.

6 It will accentuate any errors, allowing you to self-diagnose problems.

7 Yardage book poised to make notes on the breaks.

This drill will improve your putting, but it will take a little practice as it is not as easy as you might think.

FIND THE FEEL

Awareness of the clubhead weight during the stroke is crucial to putting well, but sometimes it's an easy sensation to lose.

At times when playing golf I have felt as though I have been putting with a yard broom. A simple solution is to make a few strokes holding the putter at the head end. After a dozen or so practice strokes, turn the putter round and you will instantly regain the feel of the head. I have used this trick many times during a tournament round.

CUFF IN HANDS DRILL

While endeavouring to keep my hands warm one breezy, cold morning I discovered this unusual putting drill.

I was on the putting green at Ashridge wrapped up like an Arctic explorer when I accidentally discovered the benefit of holding my right sleeve cuff in the upper part of my grip. I found that I was far more aware of my grip pressure and the instant sense of my hands working together.

ROUND THE CLOCK

This simple drill is a gem for building touch, feel and confidence. Phil Mickelson, who has one of the best touches in the world, regularly uses it.

Find a hole on your green, ideally on a slight slope, and place a dozen balls around the cup 18 inches away. Try to hole all the putts around the clock, and while doing this take into account the different breaks. Next have another trip round the clock, rolling the balls in at different speeds, knocking one in the front door, then another firmly into the back. When you are consistently holing out from this range you can extend the circle to 3 or 4 feet.

TRY BOWLING

To improve your touch, try this excellent drill, which highlights the importance of striking the ball consistently from the sweet spot.

At the Dunlop Masters in the late 1970s I watched Peter Butler, four-time Ryder Cup player, rolling putts across the practice green. He didn't seem to be holing many, but as I looked closer I realized that he wasn't even aiming at a cup. He would just send one ball across the green and then two more alongside it. What was he up to?

I found out that, rather than aim at something specific, Peter was just rolling the first ball 25–30 feet and then trying to keep his next two putts as close as possible to the first, almost like a game of bowls. Anything stroked in the same way, but slightly mishit, would come up short.

A variation of this is to hit the first ball and then attempt to hit the next ball a little further and the third one a little further again, with all three balls ending within a putter's length of each other.

It takes a good touch to get a 'toucher'.

STIMPMETER

Often when I am filming some of my 'Ken on the Course' features spectators ask why I have never explained how a Stimpmeter works, so here goes!

In 1935, after watching Gene Sarazen hit a putt off the green at the US Open at Oakmont, Edward Stimpson, who at that time was the Massachusetts Amateur Champion, was inspired to develop a way of measuring the speed of greens. He devised what was to become known as the Stimpmeter. Originally it was a piece of wood with a slot cut into it that kept a golf ball static until tipped to a certain angle that allowed the ball to run onto the green. The slot ensured the ball was always released at the same velocity, meaning you could record distances and use these to compare green speeds. Modern-day Stimpmeters are made of metal, usually 36 inches long, with ruler markings to measure how far the ball has rolled.

Here's how to use a Stimpmeter

1 Choose the flattest area on the putting surface.
2 Place a ball in the slot at the top of the Stimpmeter and tilt the ramp gently until the ball rolls out, at an angle of approximately 20 degrees.

The Stimpmeter is slowly raised until gravity starts the ball rolling down the slope.

Blue Stimpmeter with the ball resting in the slot. Green Stimpmeter showing the slot for the ball. The original Stimpmeter made by Edward Stimpson.

3 From the same spot, repeat the process with two more balls.

4 Mark the end of the Stimpmeter with a tee peg and measure from here to the average position of where the three balls finished.

5 Use the Stimpmeter, which is marked like a ruler, to measure the distance.

6 Turn around on the putting surface and repeat this testing process in the opposite direction.

7 Add the two average distances together and divide by two. For example, if the average of the first three balls is 8 feet 9 inches and then 9 feet 1 inch for the second lot of balls, the Stimpmeter reading for the green is 8 feet 11 inches. Most professional tournaments are played on greens with a Stimpmeter reading of around 10 feet 6 inches.

Understanding Stimp readings

Stimp of 6–8 feet
❍ Slow to medium pace.
❍ Ideal for all levels of golfer.
❍ Allows greenkeepers to maximize the number of pin positions.
❍ Reduces pressure on greens' maintenance, so reduces costs.
❍ Helps to speed up round times.

Stimp of 8–10 feet
❍ Manageable for all levels of handicap golfer.
❍ Perfectly fast enough for lower handicappers.
❍ Suitable for the majority of greens without pronounced contours.
❍ Ideal speed for big club competitions.

Stimp of 10–12 feet
❍ The Open Championship greens are usually 10–11 feet.

❍ Higher maintenance costs.
❍ Reduces the number of possible pin positions.
❍ Slows the pace of play for less accomplished golfers.
❍ Grass can become stressed because of long periods of cutting it so short.
❍ Strong winds may move the ball on exposed greens.

Stimp of over 12 feet
❍ Greens become very difficult to putt.
❍ Expensive and time-consuming to maintain.
❍ Some heavily contoured greens may have no 'sensible' pin positions.
❍ Exposed greens become unplayable on a windy day.
❍ Not suitable for club golf unless the greens are flat.

HOW SPEED AFFECTS
THE BREAK

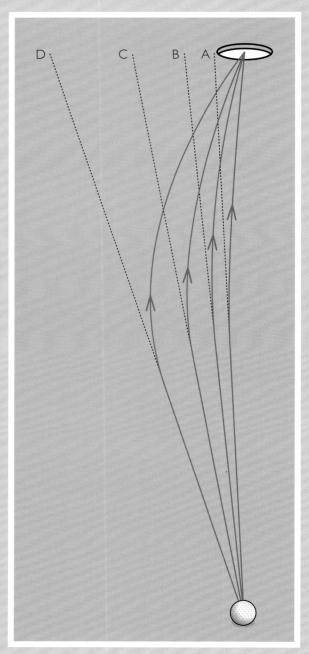

During the 1987 Ryder Cup at Muirfield Village Jack Nicklaus, US captain, got the greens up to 13 feet, believing they would be more suitable for the US team. Greens at that speed require a silky touch and a strong nerve. Just before lunch Seve and José María Olazábal in the foursomes needed two putts on the last green to win the match. Faced with a downhill 10-foot putt, Seve – with the most delicate of touches – knocked it 7 feet by, leaving Olé to famously hole the return. Big Jack was watching and realized that the greens were in danger of becoming unplayable so decided to slow them down for the afternoon session. Whatever the green speeds were going to be that year, the European team was unassailable as its members headed for their first ever victory on US soil.

This illustrates how the break is accentuated as the green speed increases:
A 6–8 feet
B 8–10 feet
C 10–12 feet
D 13 feet

FINDING THE LOST TOUCH DOWN UNDER

I first played the Australian PGA at Royal Melbourne in 1980, an Alister MacKenzie sand-belt classic. It was a course famous for its fast-running fairways and greens that made Augusta National's look tame. On arriving jet-lagged, puffy-handed and having had almost zero sun exposure for several months, I excitedly headed to the course quite unprepared for the very different conditions. The sun was so hot that as the day went by the greens gradually turned from pale green to khaki and finally a deathly-looking grey. My first practice round was worryingly disappointing. How was I going to adjust to these very different greens? It took until finishing the Pro-Am on the Wednesday to start feeling human and fully engage my brain. I headed to the practice putting green to figure out what was needed to tackle these fiendishly fast, perfectly true greens – nature's equivalent of vinyl.

I took three balls and, starting from 18 inches, I went 'round the clock' (see page 116) extending the range to 3 feet as I re-established some feel. Next, gaining a little confidence, I found the steepest slope and gently stroked some putts down the glacier from no more than 12 inches, attempting to drop the ball into the cup's front edge. Anything that missed gathered speed and ended up off the other side of the green. As my feel slowly moved into an ultra-delicate mode – my grip tension barely registering – I repeated the exercise from 18 inches, varying the pace the balls were dropping into the cup. The drill helped embed the slow, smooth rhythm and feel needed to tackle these demon greens.

The drills certainly did the trick and going into the final round of the tournament I led the field by three. Paired with Greg Norman, my hope for victory was partially dashed with a two-shot penalty for slow play ... but that's another story!

Royal Melbourne, some of the hardest and fastest greens in the world.

PUTTING AIDS

There are no real short cuts to improving your touch – it takes time and practice. A very effective place to practise is on your carpet at home. This can be simply putting to a coin or rolling some balls as close to the skirting board as you can without hitting it.

Creation 1

As a keen young amateur I tried to make my practice as effective as possible. I nipped into the woodwork room during one of my school lunch breaks and made my first putting aid using an 8-inch square of hardboard and a strip of wood rescued from the offcuts bin. It's the best ever and still used today.

One of the biggest decisions I had to make in my first house was the lounge carpet: I left the colour to my wife, and the pile to me. My choice ran true and at tournament speed I had my own 24/7

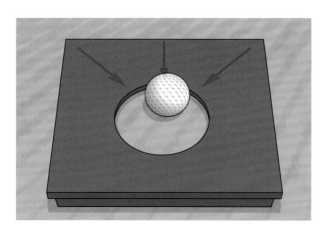

putting facility even if it was salmon-pink! If I was still playing today I would have a top-notch, artificial, indoor putting green. The very talented Tom Lewis has swapped the Axminster for one in his front room.

Creation 2

Creation No. 2 was a late 1970s' design 8 feet long with a 3½-inch hole, and used purely to improve touch and feel. You could vary the speed and break by changing the incline with the help of a couple of books.

> As little as ten minutes'
> practice a day will
> reap dividends.

Creation 3

The 1980s' model, crafted by my father-in-law from a block of hardwood and a piece of perspex, attempted to check all the putting basics:

- Head and eyes over the ball.
- Putter face 90 degrees to the aim line.
- Maintain the correct swing path.
- Swing the putter low through impact.

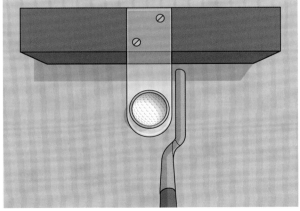

LOOKING AFTER YOUR HANDS

If your hands get too cold, putting becomes more difficult as you lose feel. Gloves and/or hand-warmers are a must in low temperatures. Conversely, in very hot weather sweaty hands can cause you to grip the putter too tightly, fearing that it may slip. Keep a small, dry hand towel in the bag.

Rickie Fowler fighting the elements at the 2011 Open.

To gain and retain a consistent sensitive touch you must keep your hands in good shape. If they become too dry there is a natural tendency to tighten your grip.

There is a very close bond between a player's hands and his or her club grips – a player will instantly recognize any unusual feel to grips. Tour players can be particularly sensitive to anybody else touching their putter grip, so as to avoid any sweaty, sun-creamed hands leaving unwelcome deposits.

Long flights can make the fingers feel puffy and so less sensitive to putting. Ben Hogan used to swear that drinking ginger ale sorted him out, while I used to dip my hands into a bucket of ice! However, ginger ale was probably more refreshing!

DARREN FINDS HIS FEEL

At the 1997 Open Championship at Royal Troon I was wandering round the practice green when Darren Clarke pulled me over and asked if I could watch him hit a few putts. This was his dilemma. He had just picked up a new putter, was about to use it for the first time and wanted to know what I thought …

He proceeded to putt with both the old faithful and new addition while I asked him some questions to hopefully steer him in the right direction and let him come to his own conclusion. 'How do you like the feel?' 'Has it got enough loft?' 'Which one feels heavier?' 'Are these links greens a little slower than the ones you are used to?' 'Try some putts with both putters from short range.' We set up a little test track to see which putter performed best from 3, 6 and 10 feet. I was beginning to get the feeling that the new purchase was becoming the favourite, but said nothing as I didn't want to influence Darren in what is a very personal and important choice. My final question was 'What is your heart telling you?'

Big Darren teed up on the Thursday morning with the shiny addition, barely out of its wrapper and never before used on a course, let alone a championship one. He putted like a demon all week, and if he hadn't knocked his tee shot at the 2nd onto the beach on the final day might well have picked up the Claret Jug instead of his runner-up cheque. He had to wait a few more years…

If you are unhappy with your putting, trying something new may just give you the little inspiration needed to get you back on track.

chapter seven

TIPS AND DRILLS

Pick the ones that work for you to keep your practice fresh, interesting and productive.

8 ONE PUTTING!

7 TIPS AND DRILLS

6 TOUCH AND FEEL

5 THE STROKE

4 THE SET-UP ROUTINE

3 READING GREENS

2 THE BASIC SET-UP

I CHOOSING A PUTTER

PLANNING YOUR PRACTICE

Before we reach the final step of the putting ladder I will share some tips and drills gleaned over my 40-plus years in professional golf. I have seen and tried dozens and chosen the best for you. They are short and simple and will help make your practice more enjoyable and productive.

Lydia Ko working on keeping her head still.

Warming up before a round is not the time to try and make any adjustments to your putting technique. This is best done at another time.

Any practice should be judged not by 'how many', but by 'how well' and ideally should last for 30–45 minutes – it is hard to concentrate fully for much longer. My dad used to say practice has to be 'constructive to be productive'; it should be challenging and fun!

If you are working on general technique it is best to keep repeating the same putt. Repetition is key to grooving the department on which you are working.

If you are prioritizing touch this is best done using just three balls: the first to give you a guide and the next two to correct any misjudgement. Repeat this from various distances.

Tiger Woods is brushing up his touch by hitting the first ball, watching how it rolls and then making any adjustments needed before he hits the next one.

In my assistant pro days at Verulam my best friend Steve Payne suggested we set ourselves a challenge to play the nine-hole putting green better ball in nine putts. We finally did it – it took 14 hours over 2 days. Some challenges really can keep you busy for a while!

Putting technique practice key points

- Don't use too many balls – six worked best for me.
- Choose a flattish smooth piece of green.
- Pick and mark a spot about 8 feet from the cup.
- Set yourself a goal of how many to hole.

THE 'KEN ON THE COURSE' ONE PUTT IMPROVER

Make your own improver; it will help with all the key aspects of your putting. It is simple, easy to make and FREE.

How to make it

○ Using the template on the opposite page, draw the shape on a piece of card.

○ Cut out with a pair of scissors.

○ Mark the card, as shown, with a felt-tip pen.

○ Cut a hole in the centre about ¼ inch in diameter.

○ Cut two holes the same size, equal distance from the centre.

How to use it

○ Aim the arrow down the line you want to start the ball on, securing the improver by pushing two tees through the holes either side of the centre.

○ Your putter head should just pass between the two tees.

○ Place a ball in the circle, allowing it to rest in the hole.

○ Use the back edge to line the putter face squarely down the arrow and your aim line.

○ Swing the head low down the arrow line.

How it will help you

○ The putter face will be square pointing down the aim line.

○ Your eyes will be directly over the ball at address if you can see the edge of the pen-marked circle on the improver.

○ The two tees help with your swing path and striking the ball from the sweet spot more consistently.

○ Before you look up make sure you can see the hole that the ball was sitting in. It will really help you keep your head still.

○ Keeping the putter grazing the arrow through impact will get the ball rolling quicker.

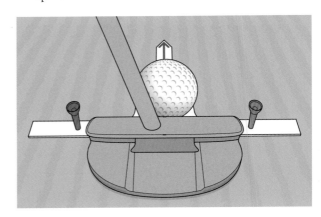

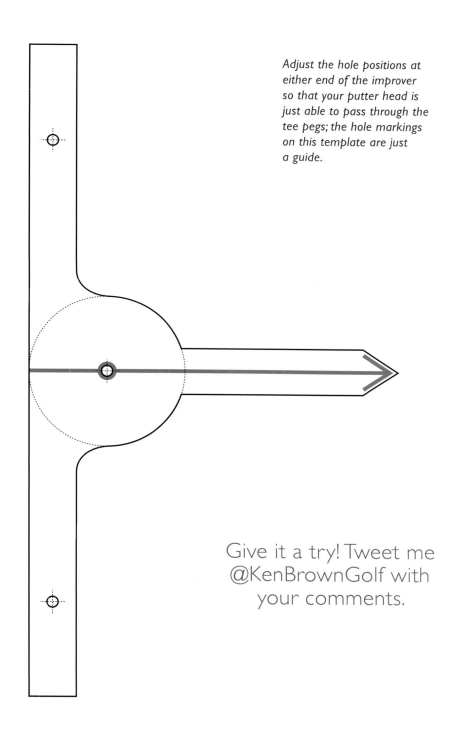

Adjust the hole positions at either end of the improver so that your putter head is just able to pass through the tee pegs; the hole markings on this template are just a guide.

Give it a try! Tweet me @KenBrownGolf with your comments.

BACK TO SCHOOL

This drill helps you get the feel of the putter shaft, left hand, wrist and forearm all working together. Such unity is essential if the putter face is consistently to return square.

Although it's important to release the putter, you don't want to let your left wrist break down through impact. Assuming you wear a watch on your left wrist, try sliding a pen or ruler inside the strap, then hit a few putts. You'll notice the pressure of the pen on the back of your left hand during the stroke; this pressure should not increase until after the ball has been hit.

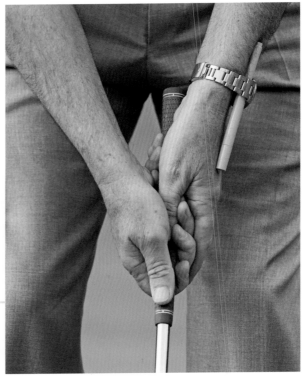

HELP FROM A HERO

When I started out Gary Player was one of my heroes. Alongside Jack Nicklaus and Arnold Palmer, he was one of the 'Big Three' featuring in a TV golf series that I watched every week, fascinated to see Gary, the little guy, win so often. Among other things he was clearly a superb putter – one of his mantras being 'head still'. Imagine aiming a gun and then, just as you pull the trigger, you move your eye. What is the chance of hitting your target? Putting is no different. Keeping your head still until the ball is on its way will work wonders. Here are some of the best tips to help:

- Hit some putts from 2 feet and, rather than watch, listen for the ball going into the cup.
- As you make contact with the ball say to yourself 'hit' – this confirms that it's safe to move your head.
- After impact, look at the grass that was under the ball – notice that it appears darker.
- Close your eye nearest the hole. This lessens the temptation to move your head while hitting.

Even the very best players have to resist the natural tendency to peek; at times they too have to work on keeping their eyes on the ball until it's hit!

Gary Player, the Black Knight with his old magic wand, still not peeking!

RESTING YOUR HEAD DRILL

Among the benefits of doing this simple drill is that it reminds you to keep your head still and eyes over the ball.

Maintaining a steady head when putting sounds much easier to achieve than it actually is. A little head movement can easily creep into your game without you even noticing!

Position your head so it just touches a wall; you will become very aware of even the slightest movement as you take your stroke. A completely still head will virtually guarantee that your eyes remain focused over the ball.

Head resting against the wall, putter flush to the skirting board.

EDGE OF GREEN DRILL

Around the perimeter of every green you will find a natural guide to check your swing path.

By swinging the putter along the slight curve of the cut line, between the green and the longer blades of the fringe, you will get an instant check-up. Remember though you must be standing on the green and not the fringe.

The edge of a green is the perfect place to have a few practice strokes – and there is one on every hole.

Using the cut line as a guide.

LONG-RANGE PUTTING

Mark James and I started on Tour together and quickly became best buddies. When playing tournaments we often finished an early supper of fish and chips and headed back to the course for half an hour's putting. Once, when I was struggling with the pace of long-range putts, Mark suggested that I stood taller to address the ball, because a more upright stance reduced the amount of wrist movement and allowed more of an 'arm swing'. I instantly started to strike the putts more solidly.

I got another tip for long-range putting from Brian Barnes, one of golf's great characters, during a practice round at St Andrews before the 1978 Open. The Old Course is famous for its large double greens, which can leave you with putts of 200 feet or more. Brian's little gem of a tip was to have the flag attended for anything more than 30–40 feet. He explained that it gave him another target to focus on, helped with his depth perception and made it a little easier to judge the speed.

The longer the putt, the further you swing the putter.

Brian Barnes, the man who beat Jack Nicklaus twice on the same day during the 1975 Ryder Cup, must be worth listening to.

PALMS TOGETHER DRILL

Rory McIlroy caught my eye a few years ago with this drill. I thought I would give it a go.

While gripping the putter between both palms, with all fingers pointing down and the forefingers running each side of the grip, I hit a few 8-foot putts across the green and quickly discovered the benefits. It really helps to get the feeling of the hands moving together, and eliminates excessive hand and wrist action. Use the drill for ten minutes and then revert to apply the feel to your stroke. If it works for Rory it is definitely worth giving it a try.

Rory has improved his technique by using this type of exercise based more on feel than mechanics.

COIN TIP

At the 1992 Open Championship played at Muirfield, Nick Faldo teased the world's media about a secret putting tip given to him by his coach David Leadbetter. It was code-named 'Basil'.

The tip made the headlines and worked well for Nick as he added his name to the Claret Jug for the third time. At the end of the week, after a little coaxing from the press, Nick revealed that 'Basil' referred to the children's television character Basil Brush. The choice of name was to remind Nick to keep the putter low to the ground and brush the grass!

The coin tip here is to check that you too are keeping the sole of the putter brushing the putting surface and keeping it low through impact. By hitting a coin instead of a ball you will make sure the clubhead is kept low to the ground at impact. This will give you the best angle of attack to achieve the optimum roll.

Sir Nick prepares to brush another putt in.

The coin tip works best on a carpet or smooth green.

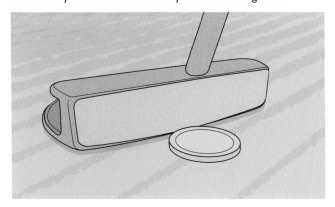

BLADED WEDGE DRILL

Take your most lofted wedge to the putting green and try to roll some balls by striking them on the equator with the leading edge.

You may struggle with this drill at first as it requires a very precise contact to get the ball rolling smoothly. With perseverance you should achieve the following:

○ Quickly become aware of any excess body movement.

○ Focus better on the precise contact point that the leading edge must strike.

○ Deliver the club to the ball at the correct angle.

○ Your hands in unison without being too wristy.

Try this drill by hitting some short-range putts, of 6 feet or under. Use the same stroke as if you are going to hit a putt.

A mishit will cause you to chip or top the ball.

TICK TOCK TIP

This is a tip that can help your timing if you find the rhythm of your stroke is getting quick or a little erratic.

Hit some putts saying 'tick' on the backswing and 'tock' on the downswing. It's that simple! You will soon find that the rhythm and pace of your stroke improve. That's a tip money can't buy!

Rory definitely got his timing right at Medinah in 2012, when he was part of the winning Ryder Cup team.

tick

tock

Luke Donald has a metronomic rhythm.

PUTTING IN THE DARK

My home course, Harpenden Common, did not have a practice putting green when I joined as a junior in 1969. The practice ground itself was only 120 yards long and practising on the course was against the rules; any putting practice had to be done out of sight of the pro, to avoid the inevitable rollocking.

One of the ways I overcame the problem was to practise at night. The second green was adjacent to a crossing of two country lanes and conveniently placed under a lamp post, which lit half the green until around midnight. There was some justice in as much as this green was about the smoothest on the course and – better still – a short cycle ride away from my house.

During my nightly forays into the shadows it quickly became evident that I was holing more short-range putts than if I were doing exactly the same in daylight. When I tried to rationalize why, I realized that in the semi-dark I was focusing much more attention on the ball and cup and not any imperfections or borrows. Therefore I was unconsciously hitting the putts firmer and more positively. The enhanced sense of hearing the ball being struck in the half light may have improved my feel.

Billy Casper, one of the truly great putters and winner of more than 50 US Tour events, told me he too used to 'night putt' as a youngster and that it had helped him considerably.

So next time you are having trouble with sleeping, don't just count sheep. Instead get up, grab your putter and head to your nearest moon-lit green. You might find that you are better at putting in the dark!

Billy Casper practising under the moonlight.

COMBATTING THE WIND

When the wind is really blowing, every part of your golf game is affected, including your putting.

For the pros, many of whom are playing golf to pay the bills, windy days can make their round a very taxing experience.

As discussed in Basic Set-up (see pages 50–71), the stability of your stance and keeping as still as you can are key factors in making a good stroke. Strong winds can seriously affect your ability to achieve this.

Key points to remember

- Widen your stance for extra stability.
- Make sure your forearms nestle into your sides to help keep your balance.
- Don't rush – it's easy to think 'I will hit between gusts.'
- Accept that you will miss some; it's the same for everyone.
- Resist the temptation to grip the putter too tightly in a vain attempt to steady your stroke.

Caddy John McLaren looks a little nervous as Duffy Waldorf putts in the wind.

THE TEXAS WEDGE

The story goes that in hot, windy Texas the fairways became so hard and dry in summer that often the best club from around the green was the putter – hence the slang term Texas wedge!

When considering your club selection from around the green the rule of thumb is always start by thinking of the club with the least loft, that is your putter, then gradually work back to the lob wedge. Generally the less time the ball is in the air the safer the shot becomes.

Next assess how the ball is lying, how far you are from the green, the state of the fairway and fringe and any borrows between the ball and the green.

'If in doubt get the putter out' is often the percentage shot, should you be in a quandary or just not feel comfortable with the choice of club.

When playing a Texas wedge it is very important to make sound contact on the ball, so it's essential to keep your head steady when making the stroke.

Rory tests his touch with a Texas wedge at the Open.

Key points to remember

- Check the line for any borrows.
- Swing a little more with the arms rather than the wrists.
- Make sure you swing the putter far enough.
- During practice rounds Tour pros would always hit a few Texas wedge shots from around a green just to test the pace of the grass on the fairways and fringes.

KEEP A SCORE

One thing all Tour players do is check their statistics, driving distance, sand saves, greens in regulation and how many putts per round.

This allows them to compare themselves with fellow competitors, see what area of their game they need to improve and, conversely, affirm what they are doing well. Keeping such a score will help you too. I suggest that whenever you take part in a competition, or any time you play with a card and pencil in hand, make a note on the scorecard of how many putts you had on each hole. You might surprise yourself. Although you may not be playing golf to pay your mortgage, such information will still motivate and guide you on how you can improve. In my early years as a pro I kept a record of every shot I played over three seasons. This mostly confirmed what I already knew, but it did reveal a few interesting facts. One was that from 3 feet and in I holed 99 per cent. Learning this helped with my confidence as I could see in black and white that there was no reason to doubt in my ability.

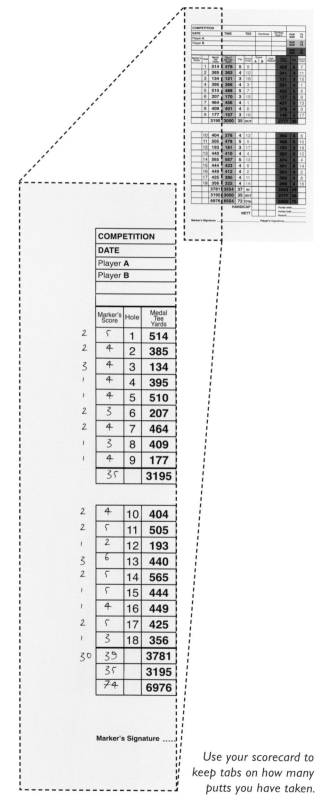

Use your scorecard to keep tabs on how many putts you have taken.

PUTTING WARM-UP

Getting a round off to a fast start builds confidence and will help you lower your score.

Before you venture out onto the course itself, hit a few warm-up putts to give you an idea of the speed and texture of the greens. Ten minutes is all it takes.

❍ Test the speed of the green by hitting a few putts of various lengths and watching how the ball rolls.

❍ Take your time when warming up; you are setting the tone for the day, so avoid rushing.

❍ Start on a flat, smooth area of the green.

❍ Hit a few short-range putts, of 2 feet to begin with; seeing the ball going into the cup is confidence-building.

❍ Try a few uphill and some downhill putts.

Tour pros honing their touch at Wentworth, the most important job of the week.

THE IMPORTANCE OF STRETCHING

Golf postures and movements are unnatural and often the cause of injury.

Occasionally after a long practice session at Ashridge Golf Club a member would catch me hanging from a tree, straightening and stretching out the old back.

After years of swinging a club with one side of my body being stretched and the other contracted, I – like many old pros – no longer have an even set of shoulders. The right shoulder is lower than the left one … be warned, stretch your back!

My right shoulder is lower than the left, caused by endless practice. STRETCH!

Post-play routine

The late Sir Henry Cotton never missed a session of 'contras' after playing golf. Basically these were a series of stretches to rebalance the body after a day crouched over the ball. Back problems affect many pro golfers, and a personal physical trainer is now regularly part of a top player's entourage. Henry was always ahead of his time.

Sir Henry, while in his 70s, still doing his regular, all-important stretches.

THE ULTIMATE FIX

Everyone has times when they just can't find the cup and their confidence is low. Struggling when on the greens is not restricted to novices. Such a feeling hits the very best too – we can all get a little nervy. If you are not sure what has gone wrong or how to put it right, work through this checklist.

1 Are you happy with your putter?

Maybe it's time for a change (see pages 14–49). This is often the first port of call for the pros. A change in your wand can inspire confidence and get those putts rolling again!

2 Is your grip worn?

This can be a licence for poor putting. Try one with a different feel (see pages 36–37). Maybe a thicker style will put you back on track.

3 Do you lack confidence?

When you are feeling a bit unsure in your play there is a natural tendency to tense up and grip the putter too tightly. Grip it lightly (see pages 56–61) and give the putter head a chance to swing.

4 Are you feeling confused?

Channel your thoughts to overcome any doubts – you can only think of one thing at a time. Use your mind to help hole the putt rather than give you a reason to miss.

Keep things simple, go back to the basics and
your One Putts will return.

5 Are you playing badly?

When Tom Lehman was having
problems on the greens he
used the mantra: 'Straight back,
straight through and roll it into the
middle of the hole.' This helped
him focus on what he needed to do.

6 Where are you looking?

Look down your aim line as if you
are looking down the barrel of a
gun and visualize the ball rolling
down the line into the hole. Make
sure you have a clear picture of
exactly where you are going to aim.

7 Go back to the basics.

Use putting aids such as my cut-out
putting improver (see page 130) to
revisit your set-up. Check your putter
face aim and that your eyes are over
the ball – remember no peeking!
This is a great check-up on the basics.

8 Are you doing your practice drills?

On the putting green build confidence
by holing short putts using a variety
of drills (see pages 128–39). Then
gradually move further away from
the hole as your putting becomes
more accurate. Confidence is king!

chapter eight

ONE PUTTING!

Practise, believe in yourself and
One Putt like the best.

LEARN FROM SIX OF THE BEST

One of the best ways of picking up pointers or developing your skills is by watching and studying people who do it the best.

Players on the board in alphabetical order:

Seve Ballesteros
Billy Casper
Hubert Green
Ben Hogan
Hale Irwin
Gene Littler
Bobby Locke
Johnny Miller
Kel Nagle
Byron Nelson
Jack Nicklaus
Andy North
Gary Player
Sam Snead
Lee Trevino
Tom Watson

As a lad I used to cut photos out of magazines and take them to the course to try and copy their techniques. It is sometimes easier to compare yourself to a photograph than a moving image, and useful to have a mental picture of what you are trying to achieve.

The following six players have consistently One Putted when they really needed to.
Let's take a look at them in action and see why...

Seve

For those who know golf, no introduction is necessary; for those who don't, no introduction is possible to Severiano Ballesteros. Among his star qualities were that he:

○ Willed the ball into the cup, and had incredible self-belief.
○ Had a simple yet stable-looking set-up.
○ Gripped the putter so lightly it looked as though it might slip out of his hands.
○ Made the putter almost comb the grass through impact.
○ Had an amazing touch ... maybe learnt from putting on the beach.
○ Retained an almost perfect line-up through the putter shaft and forearm.
○ Made this putt to win the Open Championship in 1984!

'The most important thing is to feel comfortable over the ball.'

Inbee Park

Inbee is an outstanding South Korean player and the youngest to win the US Women's Open. She has a smooth, gentle rhythm and nothing changes under pressure. In her super-human spells she holes almost everything. Among her star qualities are that she:

○ Has a smooth, steady and delicate set-up routine – no rush.

○ Has no tension in her hands, arms or shoulders; they stay loose and help give her amazing control of pace.

○ Makes no lower body movement from address to follow-through.

○ Uses a cross-handed grip with the back of her left hand pointing down her aim line.

○ Gives the feeling that she 'swings' the putter head.

'I putt by instinct and feel.'

Jack Nicklaus

If I needed someone to hole a putt for my life Jack would be my first choice. As you would expect from someone who has won 18 Majors and finished second in another 19, under pressure he was the best. Among his star qualities were that he:

○ Was a master at reading greens.

○ Had a comfortable address position with a slightly open stance.

○ With his right palm facing the target, his whole arm seemed to work like piston.

○ Used a Bristol Wizard blade putter that seemed to fit him like a glove; it had the sweet spot marked on the top edge.

○ Always kept very still over the ball.

○ Had a meticulous set-up routine, never rushing.

'I never missed a putt in my mind.'

Tiger Woods

If you want to copy someone you can do no better than Tiger Woods. His dad Earl taught him golf from 'the hole out' and it has certainly paid off. Among his star qualities are that he:

○ Performs his set-up routine with military precision.

○ Has a textbook address: stable set-up, eyes over the ball, neutral grip with the palm of the right hand facing down the aim line.

○ Uses a perfect, tension-free reverse overlap grip.

○ Works on keeping his head steady – no peeking here.

○ Uses his strength to help his stability; nothing moves that doesn't need to.

○ Always works the putter shaft, left hand and forearm together.

○ Has a gorgeous release of the clubhead!

'The best way to handle the pressure is to establish a pre-shot routine.'

Textbook Tiger

Jason Day

The Australian is one of the best putters in the game, a world No. 1 and major winner. He borrowed Tiger Woods *How I Play Golf* from his school friend, which inspired him to improve by practising in the early morning, at lunch-time and in the evening. He has retained this outstanding work ethic. Among his star qualities are that he:

○ Points his feet, knees, forearms and shoulders down the aim line.
○ Is a great visualizer of the line and pace.
○ Is the master of minimizing movement.
○ Seems to flow his lower forearms and hands into the putter shaft (see upper photo).
○ Always has his eyes over the ball.

'It's all about keeping everything steady.'

Rickie Fowler

I have always enjoyed watching Rickie Fowler putt. His stroke is so simple, natural looking and reliable. Among his star qualities are that he:

○ Hovers the putter just behind the ball for a smooth stroke.

○ Links his hands closely so that they work together.

○ Always lets the putter head swing.

○ Never moves his eyes – notice that the 'P' on his hat does not move

○ Still appears to putt with the freedom of a youngster.

'On a scale of 1–10, I want my grip pressure to be no more than 2–3.'

POSITIVE THINKING

Improving your golfing skills will reinforce your confidence, and raising your confidence will enable you to convert your practice into successful golf.

I am not a psychologist and am absolutely unqualified to sit you on the 'putting couch', but below are some tried-and-trusted ideas that might point you in the right direction to enhance your game.

○ Never give up on trying to improve your golf – good, constructive practice builds confidence.

○ Have total belief that the putter you are using is perfect for you.

○ Practise your set-up routine until your mind will not allow you to deviate in any way.

○ Visualize the line of the putt and see it going in the hole and believe that is where the ball will go.

○ Be decisive and commit with confidence. As Andy Prodger, one of the best caddies, used to say: 'Trust is a must.'

○ Decide the line and pace you are going to hit the putt and then execute it.

○ Allow yourself to blame a gust of wind or an uneven green, sweep the result under the carpet and move on to your next shot.

○ If things aren't going your way, channel your thoughts into how you want to play the next shot – champions stay in the 'here and now'; as Bobby Jones said: 'Don't allow your mind to do a little mental daisy picking.'

○ When playing in tournaments you are on your own … You have to be your own best friend.

○ If you feel nervous in competition use this to your advantage – it means you care and feel that you have the chance to do well; take a few deep breaths and believe in yourself.

And never forget you have the 19th hole … a chilled drink, bit of banter and putting any mistakes into perspective will set you up nicely for your next round!

GEORGIA PLAYS HER GAME

I first met Georgia Hall at the US Women's Open in June 2018, when her manager asked if I could have a look at her short game. I sensed that part of what was affecting her game was the transition from playing in Europe to the much bigger and busier US and so suggested meeting for dinner with Georgia and Harry, her boyfriend and caddie. We chatted a bit about her putting and I shared some of my own experiences of playing on the US Tour. I told her: 'Don't put so much pressure on yourself, play your own game and just be patient.'

I sat in on her press conference a couple of months later at the Women's British Open at Royal Lytham & St. Annes, listening to a much more confident Georgia saying 'I love links golf', that her game was 'good and the putter is warming' and that she was 'getting my head in the right place'. She came to speak to me and asked if she and Harry could join me for dinner, and if I would walk a practice round. I was delighted to do both. Over dinner she shared some of the things that helped get her head 'in the right place', explaining that her dad, Wayne, had caddied for her at the Women's British Open the previous year (where she finished third) and would be caddying for her again. Just as important as having the steps of the golfing ladder in place is filling your mind with whatever it takes to believe in yourself.

Georgia got her head in the right place and what followed was one of the most complete winning performances I had ever seen.

One putts galore!

MY BEST PUTT EVER!

It was on 14 September 1985, the Saturday of the Ryder Cup matches at the Belfry, where the lunchtime score had settled at six points all. Partnered with Bernhard Langer, Masters champion, we set off in the afternoon foursomes as the last pair out … because we were slow! The round that was to follow is forever etched on my mind.

Match strategy discussed, we decided that I should take the honour on the 1st, and we would use Bernhard's choice of ball – a lower compression Titleist than the one I played with. We had drawn two of the best Ryder Cuppers – Ray Floyd and Lanny Wadkins – on this bright, chilly and breezy day. As I prepared to hit the opening drive Bernhard summed it up: 'You just hit the fairways, I'll hit the greens and you hole the putts.' German efficiency at its best.

'Vorsprung durch Technik', all square through five holes and we had just found the 6th green in regulation. The Americans parred and Bernhard had left me a 4 footer for the half … I missed. Three putts and we were one down.

I teed off on the par-three 7th, playing straight into the teeth of the wind to a small green which had a severe slope from back to front and was almost completely surrounded by sand. Both approach shots found the front of the green, with the Americans to putt first; their putt nestled next to the hole and was conceded. Bernhard took a run at the hole to win, but missed, leaving me with 5 feet slightly downhill with a 4-inch break from the left. With an unhelpful, left-to-right, whistling wind, which had my Ryder Cup-issue trousers flapping around my legs, I could not have wished for a more uninviting putt. The green was encircled by a highly charged, expectant crowd and I was trying desperately not to think that if I missed we would be two down with two three-putts in a row and two consecutive holes given away …   could it get any worse against Ray and Lanny?

There was never a more critical time to follow the steps up the putting ladder. At that moment holing a putt was more important than oxygen. The opposition stood back and leant on their putters, gazing intently. I girded myself by going through my tried-and-tested routine, picking the line and deciding to eliminate some of the break by hitting the putt firmly. I just could not face the thought of the ball dribbling off aimlessly to the low side on the right. 'Stay still' were my last internal words … Then, gripping the putter lightly, I hit the purest putt that boldly dived right into the centre of the cup. A cheer! 'USA remain one up' was the cry of the official.

The significance of good putting was never more evident. After that 7th hole, we gained momentum, showed strong nerve to the opponents, gave ourselves a confidence boost and – most of all for me – I got a smile from Bernhard.

A few more twists and turns followed and the wind blew some good fortune our way, as we won the match three and two on the 16th. There were more than 15,000 fans thronged around the last match on the course and they lined the buggy path cheering as we were transported back to the clubhouse.

Saturday the 14th ended with Europe taking a 9–7 lead into the final day. Europe were on their way to their first Ryder Cup victory in nearly 27 years. If I had missed and we'd lost the match, it would have been 8–8 going into the singles and it might have been a different story.

One good putt can be a game changer!

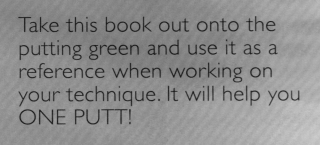

Take this book out onto the putting green and use it as a reference when working on your technique. It will help you ONE PUTT!

Play well,
Ken

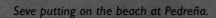

Seve putting on the beach at Pedreña.

'Golf has always been much more an art than a science
– this is certainly true when it comes to putting.'
Seve

chapter nine

PUTTING RULES

You have reached the top of the ladder. Now see how the rules can help you.

8 ONE PUTTING!

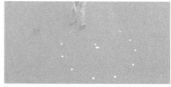

7 TIPS AND DRILLS

6 TOUCH AND FEEL

5 THE STROKE

4 THE SET-UP ROUTINE

3 READING GREENS

2 THE BASIC SET-UP

I CHOOSING A PUTTER

PUTTING RULES

It's vital that you understand what you are allowed to do on the green. Here are the key Rules:

13.1 Actions Allowed or Required on Putting Greens

This Rule allows the player to do things on the putting green that are normally not allowed off the putting green, such as being allowed to mark, lift, clean and replace a ball and to repair damage and remove sand and loose soil on the putting green. There is no penalty for accidentally causing a ball or ball-marker to move on the putting green.

13.1a When Ball Is on Putting Green

A ball is on the putting green when any part of the ball:

• Touches the putting green, or

• Lies on or in anything (such as a loose impediment or an obstruction) and is inside the edge of the putting green.

If part of the ball is both on the putting green and in another area of the course, see Rule 2.2c.

YOU CAN REPAIR DAMAGE TO THE PUTTING GREEN USING YOUR PUTTER WITHOUT PENALTY.

13.1b Marking, Lifting and Cleaning Ball on Putting Green

A ball on the putting green may be lifted and cleaned (see Rule 14.1).

The spot of the ball must be marked before it is lifted and the ball must be replaced on its original spot (see Rule 14.2).

13.1c Improvements Allowed on Putting Green

During a round and while play is stopped under Rule 5.7a, a player may take these two actions on the putting green, no matter whether the ball is on or off the putting green:

(1) Removal of Sand and Loose Soil. Sand and loose soil on the putting green (but not anywhere else on the course) may be removed without penalty.

(2) Repair of Damage. A player may repair damage on the putting green without penalty by taking reasonable actions to restore the putting green as nearly as possible to its original condition, but only:

• By using his or her hand, foot or other part of the body or a normal ball-mark repair tool, tee, club or similar item of normal equipment, and

• Without unreasonably delaying play (see Rule 5.6a).

But if the player improves the putting green by taking actions that exceed what is reasonable to restore the putting green to its original condition (such as by creating a pathway to the hole or by using an object that is not allowed), the player gets the general penalty for breach of Rule 8.1a.

'Damage on the putting green' means any damage caused by a person or outside influence, such as:

- Ball marks, shoe damage (such as spike marks) and scrapes or indentations caused by equipment or a flagstick,
- Old hole plugs, turf plugs, seams of cut turf and scrapes or indentations from maintenance tools or vehicles,
- Animal tracks or hoof indentations, and
- Embedded objects (such as a stone, acorn or tee).

But 'damage on the putting green' does not include any damage or conditions that result from:

- Normal practices for maintaining the overall condition of the putting green (such as aeration holes and grooves from vertical mowing),
- Irrigation or rain or other natural forces,

- Natural surface imperfections (such as weeds or areas of bare, diseased or uneven growth), or
- Natural wear of the hole.

14.1 Marking, Lifting and Cleaning Ball

This Rule applies to the deliberate 'lifting' of a player's ball at rest, which includes picking up the ball by hand, rotating it or otherwise deliberately causing it to move from its spot.

14.1a Spot of Ball to Be Lifted and Replaced Must Be Marked

Before lifting a ball under a Rule requiring the ball to be replaced on its original spot, the player must mark the spot which means to:

- Place a ball-marker right behind or right next to the ball, or
- Hold a club on the ground right behind or right next to the ball.

If the spot is marked with a ball-marker, after replacing the ball the player must remove the ball-marker before making a stroke.

If the player lifts the ball without marking its spot, marks its spot in a wrong way or makes a stroke with a ball-marker left in place, the player gets one penalty stroke.

If multiple Rule breaches result from a single act or related acts, see Rule 1.3c(4).

When a ball is lifted to take relief under a Rule, the player is not required to mark the spot before lifting the ball.

YOU CAN REMOVE SAND OR LOOSE SOIL WITHOUT PENALTY.

13.2 The Flagstick

This Rule covers the player's choices for dealing with the flagstick. The player may leave the flagstick in the hole or have it removed (which includes having someone attend the flagstick and remove it after the ball is played), but must decide before making a stroke. There is normally no penalty if a ball in motion hits the flagstick.

This Rule applies to a ball played from anywhere on the course, whether on or off the putting green.

13.2a Leaving Flagstick in Hole

(1) Player May Leave Flagstick in Hole. The player may make a stroke with the flagstick left in the hole, so that it is possible for the ball in motion to hit the flagstick.

The player must decide this before making the stroke, by either:

- Leaving the flagstick where it is in the hole or moving it so that it is centred in the hole and leaving it there, or

- Having a removed flagstick put back in the hole.

In either case:

- The player must not try to gain an advantage by deliberately moving the flagstick to a position other than centred in the hole.

- If the player does so and the ball in motion then hits the flagstick, he or she gets the general penalty.

13.3 Ball Overhanging Hole

13.3a Waiting Time to See if Ball Overhanging Hole Will Fall into Hole

If any part of a player's ball overhangs the lip of the hole:

- The player is allowed a reasonable time to reach the hole and ten more seconds to wait to see whether the ball will fall into the hole.

- If the ball falls into the hole in this waiting time, the player has holed out with the previous stroke.

- If the ball does not fall into the hole in this waiting time:

  ▶ The ball is treated as being at rest.

  ▶ If the ball then falls into the hole before it is played, the player has holed out with the previous stroke, but gets one penalty stroke added to the score for the hole.

UPON REACHING THE HOLE, YOU ARE ALLOWED TEN SECONDS TO SEE IF AN OVERHANGING BALL WILL DROP.

10.1b Anchoring The Club

In January 2016, the R&A and USGA changed the rules for making a putting stroke. Now, in making a stroke, the player must not anchor the club, either 'directly' or by use of an 'anchor point'.

In making a stroke, the player must not anchor the club, either:

- Directly, by holding the club or a gripping hand against any part of the body (except that the player may hold the club or a gripping hand against a hand or forearm), or

- Indirectly, through use of an 'anchor point,' by holding a forearm against any part of the body to use a gripping hand as a stable point around which the other hand may swing the club.

If the player's club, gripping hand or forearm merely touches his or her body or clothing during the stroke, without being held against the body, there is no breach of this Rule.

For the purposes of this Rule, 'forearm' means the part of the arm below the elbow joint and includes the wrist.

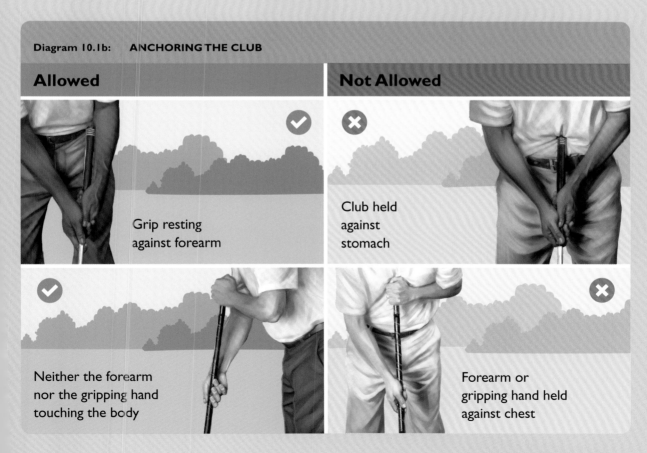

Diagram 10.1b: ANCHORING THE CLUB

Allowed

Grip resting against forearm

Neither the forearm nor the gripping hand touching the body

Not Allowed

Club held against stomach

Forearm or gripping hand held against chest

Index

Page numbers in *italics* refer to illustrations

Index

Testaments

'This is the young man most British Pros would choose to have putting for them. But it's not just natural talent that makes this lanky, young player so good; he putts and chips for three hours every day.'
Sir Henry Cotton, *Thanks for the Game*

'Ken made an immediate impact on the tour in 1976 with his lethal short game, soon gaining the nickname "One Putt". His putting method was closely examined by all and sundry, including myself. From 6 foot 2 inches he would origami himself down into a rock solid stance, the only moving part appeared to be the head of his old hickory-shafted putter. My practice times with Ken made me a better putter. I still work on his words of wisdom 40 years later and can clearly remember his bemused expression watching someone putt with so many moving parts.'
Mark James

'Over the years Ken Brown's advice has always came with authority and simplicity. On the putting green at Royal St Georges before the first round of the Open he reminded me, "let your attitude determine your golf, don't let your golf determine your attitude". My name ended up on the Claret Jug. From novice to aspiring major winner, I believe **One Putt** *will work for you.'*
Darren Clarke

'You will hole more putts and understand why by reading this book. Ken takes you step by step up the putting ladder with a simple and easy-to-follow guide, revealing all you need to One Putt. I read it, so should you.'
Lee Westwood

'I can hardly remember my own journey in golf without Ken Brown. He and I grew up playing Herts Boys' Colts and Herts County teams together through the summers of '74 and '75. He had two hallmarks; his stance and his old hickory relic putter. He had an instantly recognizable popping stroke which made that old thing work masterfully again and again. He has an easy-going and affable style, is a friend to golf and golfers on all levels and he shares his gift for putting and place in this game here. Thanks, Ken, for your friendship and the secrets shared with this book.'
Sir Nick Faldo

'Ken has brought that expertise and his considerable intellect and creativity together in One Putt, in what is the most comprehensive, entertaining and well-written book on putting you are likely to ever read.'

Brandel Chamblee

'It's no secret that I'm a keen reader, so when Ken first published One Putt I downloaded it onto my iPad and read it straight away. As well as being a great tool for instruction, it's also a fascinating insight to one of the world's best putters. Ken is highly regarded in our industry both on and off the course and for him to share some of his putting passion is nectar to golf nerds like me.'

Tommy Fleetwood

Acknowledgements

To Bill Piggott, for opening my door to professional golf, giving me the self-belief to succeed and being a wonderful friend.

Dave Cannon for his skill and patience to produce such great photos. Harpenden Common Golf Club for providing me with 50 years of sanctuary to perfect my putting and provide a beautiful backdrop for Dave's photos. Sarah Wooldridge, a wonderful lady who took me under her wing and made everything happen. Paul Wood for his technical expertise. My many friends who share my love of golf, fishing, broadcasting and laughter.

My fellow golfers, Mark James, Sir Henry Cotton, Seve, Brian Huggett, Malcolm Gregson, Sandy Lyle, Darren Clarke, Lee Westwood, Nick Faldo, Wayne Grady, Brandel Chamblee, Rory McIlroy and Tommy Fleetwood for their friendship and help with the book.

My family, Dawn, Billy and Tom, all of whom contributed their love, patience, IT skills, persistence and encouragement. One Putt would definitely not be in print without them.

An Hachette UK Company
www.hachette.co.uk

First published in Great Britain in 2015 by Hamlyn,
an imprint of Octopus Publishing Group Ltd
Carmelite House, 50 Victoria Embankment
London EC4Y 0DZ
www.octopusbooks.co.uk

Revised edition 2020

Text Copyright © Ken Brown 2015, 2020
Design and layout Copyright © Octopus Publishing Group
Ltd 2015, 2020
Rules © R&A Rules Limited

All photography David Cannon/Getty Images, with the
exception of the following:

BBC 89. **Bryce Duffy** 140. **Getty Images** Al Messerschmidt
61; Andrew Redington 60 below, 95; Augusta National 17;
ChinaPhotoPress 64 below; David Cannon/R&A 124, 125;
Don Morley 135; Harry How 154; Ian Walton/R&A 142;
Jamie Squire 94; Martyn Hayhow/AFP 141; Neil Leifer/Sports
Illustrated 133; Patrick Smith 83 left; Phil Sheldon/Popperfoto
39, 77 right, 161; Ross Kinnard 159; Sam Greenwood 82,
129; Scott Halleran 118 above; Stan Badz/PGA Tour/Getty
Images 49; Steve Powell 9; Warren Little/WME IMG 79
above left. **James Thomas Photo/iStock** 164–165. **Kevin
Murray/Octopus Publishing Group** 167 **R&A** 169.
Shutterstock tammykayphoto 87 above. **Tom Miles/
Octopus Publishing Group** 166, 168. **Toots Cotton** 145.
USGA Jonathan Kolbe 118 below.

Distributed in the US by Hachette Book Group
1290 Avenue of the Americas
4th and 5th Floors
New York, NY 10104

Distributed in Canada by Canadian Manda Group
664 Annette St.
Toronto, Ontario, Canada M6S 2C8

R&A Rules Limited and the United States Golf Association
are the joint authors and owners of the copyright in the Rules
of Golf. All rights reserved to the copyright owners. The R&A
has given Octopus Publishing Group kind permission to print
extracts from the Rules of Golf in this book.

Ken Brown asserts the moral right to be identified as the
author of this work.

ISBN 978 0 600 63644 1

A CIP catalogue record for this book is available from
the British Library

Printed and bound in China

10 9 8 7 6 5 4 3

Publishing Director: Trevor Davies
Editors: Pauline Bache & Ella Parsons
Art Director: Juliette Norsworthy
Designer: Isabel de Cordova
Assistant Production Manager: John Casey
Senior Production Manager: Peter Hunt